THE
MULTIPLICATION
WORKBOOK
FOR GRADES 3, 4, AND 5

THE MULTIPLICATION WORKBOOK FOR GRADES 3, 4, AND 5

100+ Simple Exercises and Drills to Improve Multiplication and Division

KELLY MALLOY, MS

ROCKRIDGE
PRESS

For general information on our other products and services or to obtain technical support, please contact our Customer Care Department within the United States at (866) 744-2665, or outside the United States at (510) 253-0500.

Rockridge Press publishes its books in a variety of electronic and print formats. Some content that appears in print may not be available in electronic books, and vice versa.

TRADEMARKS: Rockridge Press and the Rockridge Press logo are trademarks or registered trademarks of Callisto Media Inc. and/or its affiliates, in the United States and other countries, and may not be used without written permission. All other trademarks are the property of their respective owners. Rockridge Press is not associated with any product or vendor mentioned in this book.

Interior and Cover Designer: Jennifer Hsu
Art Producer: Meg Baggott
Editor: Andrea Leptinsky
Production Editor: Sigi Nacson
Production Manager: Michael Kay

Cover illustration © 2021 Amir Abou Roumie. Joel & Ashley Selby, 25, 117; Volyk Ievgenii/Shutterstock, 48. Author photo courtesy of Cody Malloy.

Paperback ISBN: 978-1-63807-059-7
R0

This book is dedicated to my six boys—Parker, Powell, Palmer, Tyler, Cody, and Luke—for multiplying the love!

CONTENTS

Introduction xi

How to Use This Book xiii

PART 1: GRADE 3

1   Repeated Addition 2

2   Equal Groups 4

3   Number Lines.............................. 6

Drill 1: Multiply by 1, 2, and 3 8

Fun with Math 1:
Spinning Equal Groups 9

4   Groups of Objects 10

5   Arrays and Commutative
Property 12

6   Multiply by 0 or 1 14

Drill 2: Multiply by 0, 1, 2, 3,
4, and 5 16

Fun with Math 2:
Multiplication Wheels 17

7   Multiply by 2 or 4 18

8   Multiply by 5 or 10 20

9   Multiply by 3 or 6 22

Drill 3: Multiply by 0, 1, 2, 3,
4, 5, 6, and 10 24

Fun with Math 3:
Multiplication Table Puzzle 25

10   Multiply by 7, 8, or 9 26

11   Divide by 1, 2, or 4 28

12   Divide by 5 or 10 30

Drill 4: Divide by 1, 2, 4, 5,
and 10 32

Fun with Math 4:
Roll and Color 33

13   Divide by 3 or 6 34

14   Divide by 7, 8, or 9 36

15   Relationship Between
Multiplication and Division 38

Drill 5: Divide by 1 through 10 40

Fun with Math 5: Multiplication
and Division Maze 41

PART 2: GRADE 4

1   Writing Whole Numbers in Expanded and Written Form 44

2   How 10 Relates to Place Value and Comparing Multi-Digit Numbers .. 46

3   Comparing with Multiplication 48

Drill 1: Multiplication and Division Facts 50

Fun with Math 1: Math Search 51

4   Multiplication by 10s, 100s, and 1,000s 52

5   Multi-Digit Multiplication and Area Models 54

6   Estimate Products 56

Drill 2: Multiplication and Division Facts 58

Fun with Math 2: Tile Time 59

7   Multiply with Partial Products 60

8   Remainders 62

9   Divide Multiples of 10, 100, and 1,000 64

Drill 3: Multiplication and Division Facts 66

Fun with Math 3: Mystery Picture 67

10   Division with Place Value 68

11   Division with Area Models 70

12   Estimate Quotients 72

Drill 4: Multiplication and Division 74

Fun with Math 4: Spin a Quotient 75

13   Multi-Digit Division with Partial Quotients 76

14   Multiplication and Division Word Problems 78

15   Multi-Step Word Problems 80

Drill 5: Multiplication and Division 82

Fun with Math 5: Roll and Answer 83

PART 3: GRADE 5

1   Multiply Three- and Four-Digit Numbers by Two-Digit Numbers ... 86

2   Multiply Three- and Four-Digit Numbers by Three-Digit Numbers 88

3   Multiply Multi-Digit Numbers and Assess the Reasonableness of the Product Using Estimation 90

Drill 1: Multiplication and Division Facts 92

Fun with Math 1: Weird and Random Fact 93

4   Multiplying and Dividing Whole Numbers by 10, 100, and 1,000 94

5   Divide Three-Digit Dividends by Two-Digit Divisors 96

6   Divide Four-Digit Dividends by Two-Digit and Three-Digit Divisors 98

Drill 2: Multiplication and Division Facts 100

Fun with Math 2: Math Search ..101

7   Divide Multi-Digit Numbers by One- and Two-Digit Divisors and Assess the Reasonableness of the Quotient 102

8   Multiply A One-Digit Whole Number by a Decimal 104

9   Multiply A Multi-Digit Whole Number by a Decimal 106

Drill 3: Multiplying One-Digit Whole Numbers by Decimals 108

Fun with Math 3: True or False Challenge 109

10   Multiply a Decimal by a Decimal ...110

11   Divide a Decimal by a One-Digit Whole Number 112

12   Divide a Decimal by a Two-Digit Whole Number 114

Drill 4: Dividing Decimals by Whole Numbers 116

Fun with Math 4: Decimal Fun ..117

13   Divide a Whole Number by 1 Tenth or 1 Hundredth 118

14   Divide a Whole Number or a Decimal by a Decimal 120

15   Comparing Decimal Place Values 122

Drill 5: Multiplying and Dividing One-Digit Whole Numbers by Decimals 124

Fun with Math 5: Sudoku 125

Answer Key 127

Times Table 149

Index of Skill Areas 150

INTRODUCTION

In this multiplication and division workbook for grades 3, 4, and 5, you'll find lessons, drills, and activities that will help elementary school–age children, in grades 3 through 5, practice and reinforce age-appropriate multiplication and division skills. As a third- and fourth-grade elementary teacher, I specifically designed all the materials in this book to be fun and rewarding for children to complete successfully as they build their proficiency in these important topics and gain confidence in their multiplication and division skills.

The book is divided into three parts by grade level—third grade, fourth grade, and fifth grade—and each grade level is color coded for easier use and navigation: Purple signifies activities and lessons appropriate for third graders; orange designates fourth-grade lessons and activities, and red identifies those lessons appropriate for fifth graders. Each lesson within each part progresses in difficulty, starting with easier problems to help build a child's understanding of the subject and develop confidence to tackle the more challenging problems that follow. The workbook includes a mix of multiplication and division problems, including 0 to 12 digits, mixed problems, and word problems.

Whether you're a parent, caregiver, teacher, or homeschooler of elementary school children, or other involved adult in a child's world, the lessons here give you a chance to work together at the child's pace and have fun building skills, knowledge, and confidence in multiplication and division.

Let's have some fun with math!

HOW TO USE THIS BOOK

This book is divided into three parts by grade level:

- Part 1: Grade 3
- Part 2: Grade 4
- Part 3: Grade 5

Each part focuses on the Common Core State Standards relating to multiplication and division for that specific grade and gives students a solid base to pursue more complex math instruction.

Each part offers fifteen lessons, and each lesson is followed by two practice exercises. And, although there are no "tests" in the book, the concepts taught are reinforced with a variety of fun and engaging activities, including five drills and five "Fun with Math" activities included for each grade level. As an important measure of progress and success—and to help if you're truly stumped—all answers are located at the back of the book for your convenience.

Although the book is divided by grade level, readers are welcome to move through each topic at their own pace or skip around to cover specific problems a child may need more practice with. The book and its lessons are yours to use as you see fit to increase learning, have fun, and master multiplication and division skills.

PART 1

GRADE 3

Repeated Addition

In this lesson, we will practice repeated addition. Repeated addition is adding equal groups to find the total. Multiplication is often called repeated addition. For example, in the following picture are 5 equal groups of 2.

The picture shows 5 groups of 2 pencils. If we want to know how many pencils there are altogether, we can use addition to join the equal groups. The addition sentence would be:

$2 + 2 + 2 + 2 + 2 = 10$

We can also use multiplication. Multiplication is an operation that gives the total number when you join equal groups. Because there are 5 groups of 2 pencils each, we can say "5 times 2 equals 10." The multiplication sentence would be:

$5 \times 2 = 10$

In this number sentence, the 5 and the 2 are the factors, or the numbers being multiplied. The 10 is the product, which is the answer to the multiplication problem.

Let's try an example:

2 groups of __4__

$4 + 4 =$ __8__

$2 \times$ __4__ $= 8$

One more example:

$6 + 6 + 6 + 6 =$ __4__ $\times$ __6__ $=$ __24__

PRACTICE EXERCISE 1.1

Directions: Use repeated addition to write an equation to show how many we have in each group.

1. 2 groups of ____

    ____ + ____ = ____

    2 × ____ = ____

2. 2 groups of ____

    ____ + ____ = ____

    2 × ____ = ____

3. 2 groups of ____

    ____ + ____ = ____

    2 × ____ = ____

4. 3 groups of ____

    ____ + ____ +

    ____ = ____

    3 × ____ = ____

5. 3 groups of ____

    ____ + ____ +

    ____ = ____

    3 × ____ = ____

6. 4 groups of ____

    ____ + ____ +

    ____ + ____ = ____

    4 × ____ = __

PRACTICE EXERCISE 1.2

Directions: Write out the multiplication problem using repeated addition, then solve the equation.

1. 2 × 6 = ____
2. 3 × 3 = ____
3. 4 × 2 = ____
4. 6 × 1 = ____
5. 2 × 10 = ____

6. 5 × 4 = ____
7. 4 × 4 = ____
8. 7 × 5 = ____
9. 9 × 3 = ____
10. 8 × 6 = ____

Equal Groups

In this lesson, we will practice using equal groups strategy as another way to solve multiplication problems. When creating equal groups, make sure you have the same number of items in each group.

EQUAL GROUPS

NOT EQUAL GROUPS

Remember, the two numbers you are going to multiply are called the factors. The factors determine how many groups you make, and how many equal items are in each group.

The commutative property of multiplication says that you can switch the order of the factors and still get the same product, or answer, to a multiplication problem. So 4 × 6 = 24 and 6 × 4 = 24.

When using the equal groups strategy, you can use almost anything to represent the items in your group. For this lesson we are going to represent the groups as medium-size circles, and the items within the groups are dots. We use circles and dots because they are quick and easy to make. It can be helpful to fill in your dots like a tens frame to make it easier to count.

Let's try an example:

6 × 3 = ___

This means we have 6 groups, with 3 items in each group.

If we count all the items, we see that the product is 18: 6 × 3 = 18.

PRACTICE EXERCISE 2.1

Directions: Write a multiplication sentence to match the models shown.

1. _____ × _____ = _____

2. _____ × _____ = _____

3. _____ × _____ = _____

4. _____ × _____ = _____

5. _____ × _____ = _____

PRACTICE EXERCISE 2.2

Directions: Use the equal groups strategy to solve the following word problems.

1. Max has 5 shoeboxes. Each box contains 2 shoes. How many shoes does Max have?

2. Alan donated 3 packages of socks. Each package had 6 pairs of socks in it. How many pairs of socks did Alan donate?

3. Sarah has 4 cats. She gave each cat 3 treats. How many treats did Sarah give out?

4. The librarian received a delivery of 5 boxes. Each box had 6 books in it. How many books did the librarian receive?

5. Lucy had 7 containers of tennis balls. Each container had 3 tennis balls in it. How many tennis balls did Lucy have?

Number Lines

In this lesson, we will practice using a number line as a tool to help us multiply two factors. A number line is a line divided into equal units that are numbered in order. You can show multiplication on a number line. We multiply by drawing jumps on the number line. Each arrow represents one jump on the number line.

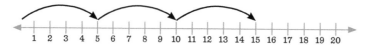

Here, 3 jumps of 5 shows 3 groups of 5. The last number we land on is the product, or answer, to a multiplication problem:

$3 \times 5 = 15$

Let's try an example:

$4 \times 2 =$ ___

In this problem, there are 4 groups of 2. Using a number line, we are going to make 4 jumps of 2.

The last number we landed on is 8, so $4 \times 2 = 8$.
Let's try another example:

$3 \times 6 =$ ___

In this problem, there are 3 groups of 6. Using a number line, we are going to make 3 jumps of 6.

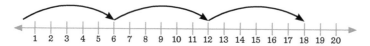

The last number we landed on is 18, so $3 \times 6 = 18$.

PRACTICE EXERCISE 3.1

Directions: Draw the hops on each number line and complete the multiplication sentences.

1. 5 × 2 = _____

   1 2 3 4 5 6 7 8 9 10 11 12 13 14 15 16 17 18 19 20

2. 4 × 3 = _____

   1 2 3 4 5 6 7 8 9 10 11 12 13 14 15 16 17 18 19 20

3. 2 × 4 = _____

   1 2 3 4 5 6 7 8 9 10 11 12 13 14 15 16 17 18 19 20

4. 3 × 5 = _____

   1 2 3 4 5 6 7 8 9 10 11 12 13 14 15 16 17 18 19 20

5. 9 × 2 = _____

   1 2 3 4 5 6 7 8 9 10 11 12 13 14 15 16 17 18 19 20

PRACTICE EXERCISE 3.2

Directions: Draw the hops on each number line and complete the multiplication sentences.

1. 6 × 3 = _____

   1 2 3 4 5 6 7 8 9 10 11 12 13 14 15 16 17 18 19 20

2. 5 × 3 = _____

   1 2 3 4 5 6 7 8 9 10 11 12 13 14 15 16 17 18 19 20

3. 3 × 3 = _____

   1 2 3 4 5 6 7 8 9 10 11 12 13 14 15 16 17 18 19 20

4. 2 × 7 = _____

   1 2 3 4 5 6 7 8 9 10 11 12 13 14 15 16 17 18 19 20

5. 8 × 1 = _____

   1 2 3 4 5 6 7 8 9 10 11 12 13 14 15 16 17 18 19 20

MULTIPLY BY 1, 2, AND 3

Name: _____ Time: _____

100%

Directions: Find the product for each problem.

1. $\begin{array}{r} 1 \\ \times\,1 \\ \hline 1 \end{array}$	2. $\begin{array}{r} 2 \\ \times\,1 \\ \hline 2 \end{array}$	3. $\begin{array}{r} 1 \\ \times\,3 \\ \hline 3 \end{array}$	4. $\begin{array}{r} 2 \\ \times\,2 \\ \hline 4 \end{array}$	5. $\begin{array}{r} 2 \\ \times\,3 \\ \hline 6 \end{array}$
6. $\begin{array}{r} 3 \\ \times\,1 \\ \hline 3 \end{array}$	7. $\begin{array}{r} 3 \\ \times\,2 \\ \hline 6 \end{array}$	8. $\begin{array}{r} 2 \\ \times\,2 \\ \hline 4 \end{array}$	9. $\begin{array}{r} 1 \\ \times\,6 \\ \hline 6 \end{array}$	10. $\begin{array}{r} 1 \\ \times\,7 \\ \hline 7 \end{array}$
11. $\begin{array}{r} 2 \\ \times\,4 \\ \hline 8 \end{array}$	12. $\begin{array}{r} 3 \\ \times\,4 \\ \hline 12? \end{array}$	13. $\begin{array}{r} 3 \\ \times\,3 \\ \hline 9 \end{array}$	14. $\begin{array}{r} 1 \\ \times\,4 \\ \hline 4 \end{array}$	15. $\begin{array}{r} 2 \\ \times\,5 \\ \hline 10 \end{array}$
16. $\begin{array}{r} 3 \\ \times\,5 \\ \hline 13 \end{array}$	17. $\begin{array}{r} 3 \\ \times\,6 \\ \hline 18 \end{array}$	18. $\begin{array}{r} 1 \\ \times\,8 \\ \hline 8 \end{array}$	19. $\begin{array}{r} 3 \\ \times\,4 \\ \hline 12? \end{array}$	20. $\begin{array}{r} 3 \\ \times\,5 \\ \hline 15 \end{array}$
21. $\begin{array}{r} 1 \\ \times\,1 \\ \hline 1 \end{array}$	22. $\begin{array}{r} 1 \\ \times\,8 \\ \hline 8 \end{array}$	23. $\begin{array}{r} 2 \\ \times\,6 \\ \hline 12 \end{array}$	24. $\begin{array}{r} 2 \\ \times\,7 \\ \hline 14 \end{array}$	25. $\begin{array}{r} 3 \\ \times\,7 \\ \hline 21 \end{array}$
26. $\begin{array}{r} 2 \\ \times\,8 \\ \hline 16 \end{array}$	27. $\begin{array}{r} 1 \\ \times\,9 \\ \hline 9 \end{array}$	28. $\begin{array}{r} 3 \\ \times\,8 \\ \hline 24? \end{array}$	29. $\begin{array}{r} 3 \\ \times\,10 \\ \hline 30 \end{array}$	30. $\begin{array}{r} 2 \\ \times\,10 \\ \hline 20 \end{array}$

SPINNING EQUAL GROUPS

Directions: Use a paper clip and a pencil to spin the first spinner to find your number of groups. Spin the second spinner to find the number of dots you will put inside each group. Write your number sentences and solve to find the product.

GROUPS

EACH

Groups of Objects

We talked about using groups of objects to solve multiplication problems in Lesson 2 (page 4). In this lesson, we will talk again about using groups of objects to solve multiplication problems. Try this challenge: How many dots are there?

We see that there are three groups and that each group has four dots in it. There are 12 dots total if we add $4 + 4 + 4 = 12$. We can also use the multiplication sentence $4 \times 3 = 12$, or 4 groups of 3 equals 12.

Let's try an example:

What multiplication sentence could you write about these groups?

First, we need to see how many groups there are. There are 8 groups. The next thing we need to know is how many dots are in each group. There are 2 dots in each group. We can use the multiplication sentence $8 \times 2 = 16$.

One more example:

What multiplication sentence could you write about these groups?

First, we need to see how many groups there are. There are 5 groups. The next thing we need to know is how many dots are in each group. There are 6 dots in each group. We can use the multiplication sentence $5 \times 6 = 30$.

PRACTICE EXERCISE 4.1

Directions: Write a multiplication sentence to describe each following group.

1. _____ × _____ = _____

2. _____ × _____ = _____

3. _____ × _____ = _____

Directions: Draw equal groups to find the answer to each multiplication sentence.

4. $3 \times 4 =$

5. $2 \times 6 =$

PRACTICE EXERCISE 4.2

Directions: Draw equal groups to find the answer to each multiplication sentence.

1. $4 \times 5 =$ _____

2. $7 \times 3 =$ _____

3. $6 \times 4 =$ _____

Directions: Write a multiplication sentence to describe each following group.

4. _____ × _____ = _____

5. _____ × _____ = _____

Arrays and Commutative Property

An array is a set of objects that are arranged in rows and columns. In this lesson, we will learn to use arrays to model multiplication and find factors.

The commutative property of multiplication says you can switch the order of the factors and still get the same product, or answer, to a multiplication problem. Because of the commutative property, we can arrange the same number of objects in a different array and find the same product.

Let's try an example:

What multiplication sentence could you write about this array?

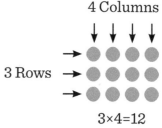

3 Columns

4 Rows

4×3=12

4 Columns

3 Rows

3×4=12

★ ★ ★   _2_ rows of _3_ = _6_

★ ★ ★   _2_ × _3_ = _6_

One more example:

What multiplication sentence could you write about this array?

▲ ▲ ▲ ▲   _4_ rows of _4_ = _16_

▲ ▲ ▲ ▲   _4_ × _4_ = _16_

▲ ▲ ▲ ▲

▲ ▲ ▲ ▲

PRACTICE EXERCISE 5.1

Directions: Write a multiplication sentence to describe each following array.

1. ____ row(s) of ____ = ____

   ____ × ____ = ____

2. ____ row(s) of ____ = ____

   ____ × ____ = ____

3. ____ row(s) of ____ = ____

   ____ × ____ = ____

4. ____ row(s) of ____ = ____

   ____ × ____ = ____

5. ____ row(s) of ____ = ____

   ____ × ____ = ____

PRACTICE EXERCISE 5.2

Directions: Create an array for each multiplication sentence, then find the product.

1. 2 × 8 =	2. 5 × 5 =	3. 4 × 8 =
4. 3 × 9 =	5. 5 × 1 =	6. 4 × 5 =

Multiply by 0 or 1

In this lesson, we will practice multiplying by 0 or 1. When we multiply by 0 or by 1, we may see some patterns that will help us whenever we multiply by either factor.

For example, if we multiply 1×4, this means 1 group of 4.

$1 \times 4 = 4$

Likewise, if we were to multiply 1×2, the total is 2.

$1 \times 2 = 2$

You may notice that the product is the same as the factor that is not 1. This is called the identity property, which states that the product of 1 and any number is that number.

If we switch the factors around using the commutative property, we see that the product is still the same.

$2 \times 1 = 2$

2 groups of 1 has the same product as 1 group of 2.

Now let's take a look at what happens when we multiply by 0.

$4 \times 0 = $ ____

We ask, "What does this mean?" It means we have 4 groups of 0, so the answer is $4 \times 0 = 0$.

You may notice that when we multiply a number by zero, the product is zero. This is called the zero property of multiplication, which states that the product of 0 and any number is 0.

Let's try an example:

$5 \times 1 = 5$

One more example:

$0 \times 9 = 0$

PRACTICE EXERCISE 6.1

Directions: Solve the following multiplication facts.

1. $5 \times 0 =$ _____

2. $3 \times 0 =$ _____

3. $6 \times 0 =$ _____

4. $0 \times 8 =$ _____

5. $0 \times 7 =$ _____

6. $0 \times 3 =$ _____

7. There are 3 baskets at the register, each containing 0 items. How many items are there in all?

8. There are 7 empty plates on the counter. How many cookies are on the plates?

PRACTICE EXERCISE 6.2

Directions: Solve the following multiplication facts.

1. $1 \times 4 =$ _____

2. $2 \times 1 =$ _____

3. $9 \times 1 =$ _____

4. $1 \times 7 =$ _____

5. $1 \times 0 =$ _____

6. $4 \times 1 =$ _____

7. Mari has 1 package of pencils with 10 pencils inside. How many pencils are there in all?

8. There is 1 plate on the counter with 6 cookies on it. How many cookies are there in all?

MULTIPLY BY 0, 1, 2, 3, 4, AND 5

Name: _____ Time: _____

Directions: Find the product for each.

1. $\begin{array}{r} 3 \\ \times 1 \\ \hline \end{array}$	2. $\begin{array}{r} 10 \\ \times 0 \\ \hline \end{array}$	3. $\begin{array}{r} 1 \\ \times 3 \\ \hline \end{array}$	4. $\begin{array}{r} 8 \\ \times 1 \\ \hline \end{array}$	5. $\begin{array}{r} 5 \\ \times 5 \\ \hline \end{array}$
6. $\begin{array}{r} 2 \\ \times 5 \\ \hline \end{array}$	7. $\begin{array}{r} 0 \\ \times 3 \\ \hline \end{array}$	8. $\begin{array}{r} 4 \\ \times 10 \\ \hline \end{array}$	9. $\begin{array}{r} 5 \\ \times 6 \\ \hline \end{array}$	10. $\begin{array}{r} 1 \\ \times 6 \\ \hline \end{array}$
11. $\begin{array}{r} 2 \\ \times 1 \\ \hline \end{array}$	12. $\begin{array}{r} 4 \\ \times 1 \\ \hline \end{array}$	13. $\begin{array}{r} 3 \\ \times 3 \\ \hline \end{array}$	14. $\begin{array}{r} 2 \\ \times 4 \\ \hline \end{array}$	15. $\begin{array}{r} 1 \\ \times 5 \\ \hline \end{array}$
16. $\begin{array}{r} 3 \\ \times 3 \\ \hline \end{array}$	17. $\begin{array}{r} 3 \\ \times 5 \\ \hline \end{array}$	18. $\begin{array}{r} 7 \\ \times 1 \\ \hline \end{array}$	19. $\begin{array}{r} 0 \\ \times 4 \\ \hline \end{array}$	20. $\begin{array}{r} 5 \\ \times 2 \\ \hline \end{array}$
21. $\begin{array}{r} 7 \\ \times 1 \\ \hline \end{array}$	22. $\begin{array}{r} 2 \\ \times 2 \\ \hline \end{array}$	23. $\begin{array}{r} 7 \\ \times 2 \\ \hline \end{array}$	24. $\begin{array}{r} 4 \\ \times 10 \\ \hline \end{array}$	25. $\begin{array}{r} 0 \\ \times 4 \\ \hline \end{array}$
26. $\begin{array}{r} 1 \\ \times 8 \\ \hline \end{array}$	27. $\begin{array}{r} 2 \\ \times 9 \\ \hline \end{array}$	28. $\begin{array}{r} 1 \\ \times 8 \\ \hline \end{array}$	29. $\begin{array}{r} 3 \\ \times 0 \\ \hline \end{array}$	30. $\begin{array}{r} 4 \\ \times 3 \\ \hline \end{array}$

MULTIPLICATION WHEELS

Directions: Multiply each number on the wheel by the number in the center and write in your answer like the examples shown.

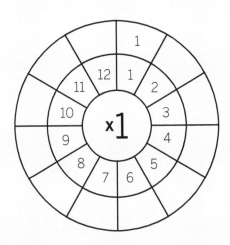

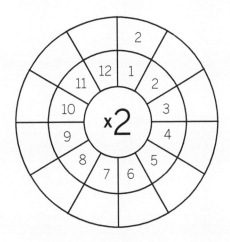

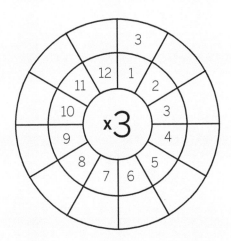

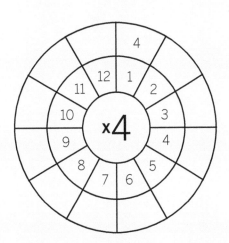

Multiply by 2 or 4

In this lesson, we will practice multiplying by 2 or 4. Multiplying by 2 is the same as doubling the other factor, or number, in the equation. If we have 2 groups of 3, or 2×3, we can think of it as doubling the 3 or $3 + 3 = 6$.

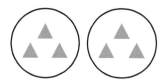

$2 \times 3 = 6$

When we multiply by 4, we can double the other factor (multiply by 2) and then double the product.

So, if we have 4 groups of 3, or 4×3, we first double the other number (3), so $2 \times 3 = 6$. Then we double the product (6), so 2×6, or $6 + 6 = 12$. The product of $4 \times 3 = 12$.

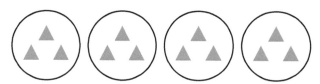

Let's try an example:

$5 \times 2 = $ ____

When we multiply by 2, we can double the other factor. So we can use $5 + 5 = 10$ to find the product: $5 \times 2 = 10$.

Let's try 9×4. When we multiply by 4, we double the other number, then double the product. We can use $9 + 9 = 18$. Then we double the product $18 + 18 = 36$, so $9 \times 4 = 36$.

PRACTICE EXERCISE 7.1

Directions: Solve the following multiplication facts.

1. 3 × 2 = _____

2. 2 × 2 = _____

3. 2 × 5 = _____

4. 2 × 6 = _____

5. 2 × 7 = _____

6. 2 × 9 = _____

7. Marcus has 2 dogs. He feeds them each 8 cups of food a week. How many cups of food did Marcus feed the dogs in all?

8. One bag of apples weighs 4 pounds. How much do 2 bags of apples weigh?

PRACTICE EXERCISE 7.2

Directions: Solve the following multiplication facts.

1. 4 × 2 = _____

2. 4 × 6 = _____

3. 4 × 3 = _____

4. 4 × 8 = _____

5. 4 × 3 = _____

6. 4 × 7 = _____

7. Rachel's mom bought 4 pounds of chicken for $3.00 per pound. How much did she spend for the chicken?

8. Luke invited 8 friends to his birthday party. He put 4 candies in each of their party bags. How many candies did Luke give out?

Multiply by 5 or 10

In this lesson, we will practice multiplying by 5 or 10. Similar to how we multiply by other numbers, there are patterns when we multiply by 5 and 10. When we multiply by 10, we can skip count by tens.

In this array, we have 4 groups of 10. To find 4 × 10, we can skip count by ten four times: 10, 20, 30, 40, so 4 × 10 = 40.

When we multiply by 5, we can skip count by fives.

In this array, we have 4 groups of 5. To find 4 × 5, we can skip count by five four times: 5, 10, 15, 20, so 4 × 5 = 20.

You may have noticed that when we multiplied by 5, the product was one-half of the product that we got when we multiplied by 10. That is because half of 10 = 5. We can use that strategy as well.

For example, if we are trying to find the product of 5 × 6, we can first find the product of 10 × 6 by skip counting by ten six times: 10, 20, 30, 40, 50, 60. We then find half of the product: half of 60 is 30, so 5 × 6 = 30.

PRACTICE EXERCISE 8.1

Directions: Solve the following multiplication facts.

1. 10 × 1 = _____

2. 10 × 3 = _____

3. 10 × 6 = _____

4. 10 × 2 = _____

5. 10 × 7 = _____

6. 10 × 8 = _____

7. A volunteer group is planting trees in 5 parks. If they plant 10 trees in each park, how many trees do they plant in all?

8. The volunteer group is also planting flowers. If they plant 10 flowers in 7 different flower beds, how many flowers do they plant in all?

PRACTICE EXERCISE 8.2

Directions: Solve the following multiplication facts.

1. 5 × 3 = _____

2. 5 × 1 = _____

3. 5 × 6 = _____

4. 5 × 5 = _____

5. 5 × 4 = _____

6. 5 × 9 = _____

7. Emily watched 8 YouTube videos. Each video was 5 minutes long. How long did Emily spend watching videos?

8. Arturo has 3 bills in his wallet and each is a $5 bill. How much money does Arturo have?

9

Multiply by 3 or 6

In this lesson, we will practice multiplying by 3 or 6. When we multiply by 3, we can start by thinking of the double of a number, then add one more set.

2 × 6 +6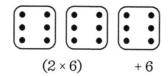

(2 × 6)   + 6

For example, if we are trying to solve 3 × 6, we can start with 2 × 6 = 12. Then we just add one more set of 6: 12 + 6 = 18, so 3 × 6 = 18.

When we multiply by 6, we can first multiply by 3 and then double the product. If we want to multiply 6 × 6, we first find 3 × 6 = 18. Then we can double the product: 18 + 18 = 36, so 6 × 6 = 36.

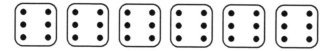

Let's try an example:

4 × 3 = ____

First, we multiply 4 × 2 = 8, then we add one more group of 4: 8 + 4 = 12, so 4 × 3 = 12.

(2 × 4) +4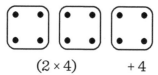

(2 × 4)   + 4

One more example:

4 × 6 = ____

First, we find 3 × 4 = 12, then we double the product: 12 + 12 = 24, so 4 × 6 = 24.

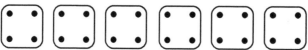

PRACTICE EXERCISE 9.1

Directions: Solve the following multiplication facts.

1. 3 × 2 = _____

2. 3 × 3 = _____

3. 5 × 3 = _____

4. 10 × 3 = _____

5. 3 × 7 = _____

6. 3 × 9 = _____

7. A teacher put 3 pencils in each of 5 pouches. How many pencils did the teacher use in all?

8. There are 3 boxes with 9 cupcakes in each box. How many cupcakes are there in all?

PRACTICE EXERCISE 9.2

Directions: Solve the following multiplication facts.

1. 6 × 1 = _____

2. 6 × 2 = _____

3. 6 × 4 = _____

4. 6 × 6 = _____

5. 6 × 8 = _____

6. 6 × 10 = _____

7. There are 5 carriages on an amusement park ride. Each carriage carries 6 people. How many people can go on the ride at once?

8. Marco bought 6 packages of cookies. Each package contained 8 cookies. How many cookies did Marco have to share?

MULTIPLY BY 0, 1, 2, 3, 4, 5, 6, AND 10

Name: _____ Time: _____

Directions: Find the product for each problem.

1. 0 ×1	2. 10 ×3	3. 4 ×3	4. 8 ×2	5. 7 ×5
6. 2 ×9	7. 6 ×3	8. 6 ×10	9. 5 ×4	10. 3 ×6
11. 2 ×7	12. 4 ×6	13. 8 ×3	14. 4 ×4	15. 3 ×5
16. 6 ×5	17. 3 ×6	18. 7 ×10	19. 6 ×4	20. 5 ×6
21. 6 ×6	22. 4 ×2	23. 6 ×7	24. 2 ×10	25. 8 ×4
26. 2 ×8	27. 2 ×7	28. 3 ×8	29. 6 ×0	30. 4 ×8

MULTIPLICATION TABLE PUZZLE

Directions: Find the value of each food in the following multiplication table. The puzzle works like a multiplication table: You multiply the factors listed above each column by the factors in the rows to find the value listed in the table where they meet. For example, 2 × 6 = 12, so the apple has a value of 12.

Multiply by 7, 8 or 9

In this lesson, we will practice multiplying by 7, 8, or 9. To do this, we can use a break-apart strategy to break down the factor into smaller factors that we already know how to multiply.

Let's try an example: We want to multiply 7×4. First, break apart the factor 7 into 5 and 2. We then multiply $5 \times 4 = 20$, then $2 \times 4 = 8$. We add the two products together to solve for 7×4: $20 + 8 = 28$, so $7 \times 4 = 28$.

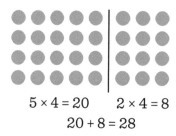

$5 \times 4 = 20 \qquad 2 \times 4 = 8$

$20 + 8 = 28$

Let's try another one: $8 \times 6 =$ ____

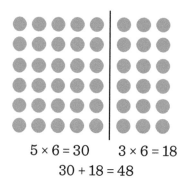

$5 \times 6 = 30 \qquad 3 \times 6 = 18$

$30 + 18 = 48$

We can break apart the factor 8 into 5 and 3. We then multiply $5 \times 6 = 30$ and $3 \times 6 = 18$. We add the two products together to solve for 8×6: $30 + 18 = 48$, so $8 \times 6 = 48$.

PRACTICE EXERCISE 10.1

Directions: Solve the following multiplication facts.

1. $3 \times 7 =$ _____

2. $8 \times 3 =$ _____

3. $7 \times 6 =$ _____

4. $8 \times 4 =$ _____

5. $8 \times 6 =$ _____

6. $7 \times 9 =$ _____

7. A teacher put 8 pencils in each of 5 pouches. How many pencils did the teacher use in all?

8. Mia's karate school has 4 classes every day with 9 students in each class. How many students go to Mia's karate school each day?

PRACTICE EXERCISE 10.2

Directions: Solve the following multiplication facts.

1. $4 \times 7 =$ _____

2. $8 \times 7 =$ _____

3. $7 \times 7 =$ _____

4. $9 \times 4 =$ _____

5. $8 \times 8 =$ _____

6. $9 \times 9 =$ _____

7. Smiley's doughnuts sells doughnuts in boxes of 9. If they sell 6 boxes, how many doughnuts do they sell in all?

8. An aquarium has 8 fish tanks with 6 fish in each tank. How many fish does the aquarium have?

Divide by 1, 2, or 4

In this lesson, we will practice dividing by 1, 2, or 4. Just as we can use patterns when we multiply, we can also use patterns when we divide. When we multiplied by 1, the product was the other factor. When we divide by 1, the quotient, or answer, will also be the other number. So, for example, $8 \div 1 = 8$.

Also, when we divide a factor by itself, the answer, or quotient, will be 1.

When we divide by 2, we divide the whole amount by 2 equally. You will notice that the answer is the same as half of the dividend, or the whole amount we are dividing.

$8 \div 2 = 4$

We can see that 4 is half of 8.

When we divide by 4, we can first divide by 2 and then divide the quotient, or the answer, by 2 again.

$8 \div 4 = \underline{\quad}$

We first divide 8 by 2, or $8 \div 2 = 4$. Then we divide the quotient, or answer, by 2, or $4 \div 2 = 2$.

PRACTICE EXERCISE 11.1

Directions: Solve the following division facts.

1. 3 ÷ 1 = _____

2. 8 ÷ 2 = _____

3. 4 ÷ 4 = _____

4. 10 ÷ 2 = _____

5. 12 ÷ 4 = _____

6. 16 ÷ 4 = _____

7. There are some bicycles at the bike rack. If there are 12 wheels, how many bicycles are there?

8. Jacob is reading a book and has 16 pages left to read. If Jacob reads 4 pages every day, how many days will it take him to read the book?

PRACTICE EXERCISE 11.2

Directions: Solve the following division facts.

1. 8 ÷ 1 = _____

2. 16 ÷ 2 = _____

3. 1 ÷ 1 = _____

4. 18 ÷ 2 = _____

5. 24 ÷ 4 = _____

6. 36 ÷ 4 = _____

7. You have 16 cookies that you want to share equally with 4 people. How many cookies does each person get?

8. Tyler bought 4 posters for $12. How much did he spend for each poster?

Divide by 5 or 10

In this lesson, we will practice dividing by 5 or 10. Dividing by 5 means we split the number into 5 equal groups, so there are 5 in each group.

If we have 20 items and want to divide them into 5 equal groups, we can skip count by fives—5, 10, 15, 20—to find that we can put 4 into each group.

Dividing by 10 means we split the number into 10 equal groups, so that there are 10 in each group. If we have 20 items, and we want to divide them into 10 equal groups, we can skip count by tens—10, 20—and see that there are 2 in each group.

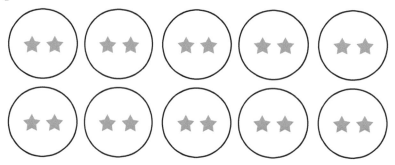

PRACTICE EXERCISE 12.1

Directions: Solve the following division facts.

1. $5 \div 5 =$ _____

2. $15 \div 5 =$ _____

3. $10 \div 5 =$ _____

4. $20 \div 5 =$ _____

5. $35 \div 5 =$ _____

6. $45 \div 5 =$ _____

7. Coach Ramirez has 50 baseballs. If Coach can fit 5 baseballs in 1 box, how many boxes does Coach need to carry all the baseballs?

8. A small milk container has 5 ounces of milk in it. If there are 25 ounces of milk on the table, how many containers are there?

PRACTICE EXERCISE 12.2

Directions: Solve the following division facts.

1. $10 \div 1 =$ _____

2. $10 \div 10 =$ _____

3. $30 \div 10 =$ _____

4. $50 \div 10 =$ _____

5. $70 \div 10 =$ _____

6. $100 \div 10 =$ _____

7. There are 80 players divided evenly into 10 teams. How many players are on each team?

8. A sandwich shop can make 10 sandwiches in 1 hour. How many hours will it take to make 60 sandwiches?

DIVIDE BY 1, 2, 4, 5, AND 10

Name: _____ Time: _____

Directions: Find the quotient for each.

1. $\begin{array}{r} 2 \\ \div 2 \\ \hline \end{array}$	2. $\begin{array}{r} 6 \\ \div 2 \\ \hline \end{array}$	3. $\begin{array}{r} 5 \\ \div 1 \\ \hline \end{array}$	4. $\begin{array}{r} 12 \\ \div 2 \\ \hline \end{array}$	5. $\begin{array}{r} 8 \\ \div 2 \\ \hline \end{array}$
6. $\begin{array}{r} 10 \\ \div 2 \\ \hline \end{array}$	7. $\begin{array}{r} 8 \\ \div 4 \\ \hline \end{array}$	8. $\begin{array}{r} 12 \\ \div 4 \\ \hline \end{array}$	9. $\begin{array}{r} 5 \\ \div 5 \\ \hline \end{array}$	10. $\begin{array}{r} 24 \\ \div 4 \\ \hline \end{array}$
11. $\begin{array}{r} 20 \\ \div 10 \\ \hline \end{array}$	12. $\begin{array}{r} 25 \\ \div 5 \\ \hline \end{array}$	13. $\begin{array}{r} 16 \\ \div 2 \\ \hline \end{array}$	14. $\begin{array}{r} 16 \\ \div 4 \\ \hline \end{array}$	15. $\begin{array}{r} 30 \\ \div 10 \\ \hline \end{array}$
16. $\begin{array}{r} 9 \\ \div 1 \\ \hline \end{array}$	17. $\begin{array}{r} 20 \\ \div 5 \\ \hline \end{array}$	18. $\begin{array}{r} 20 \\ \div 4 \\ \hline \end{array}$	19. $\begin{array}{r} 30 \\ \div 5 \\ \hline \end{array}$	20. $\begin{array}{r} 25 \\ \div 5 \\ \hline \end{array}$
21. $\begin{array}{r} 30 \\ \div 2 \\ \hline \end{array}$	22. $\begin{array}{r} 20 \\ \div 2 \\ \hline \end{array}$	23. $\begin{array}{r} 28 \\ \div 4 \\ \hline \end{array}$	24. $\begin{array}{r} 50 \\ \div 10 \\ \hline \end{array}$	25. $\begin{array}{r} 18 \\ \div 2 \\ \hline \end{array}$
26. $\begin{array}{r} 32 \\ \div 4 \\ \hline \end{array}$	27. $\begin{array}{r} 40 \\ \div 4 \\ \hline \end{array}$	28. $\begin{array}{r} 40 \\ \div 10 \\ \hline \end{array}$	29. $\begin{array}{r} 60 \\ \div 10 \\ \hline \end{array}$	30. $\begin{array}{r} 50 \\ \div 5 \\ \hline \end{array}$

ROLL AND COLOR

Directions: Each player chooses a different-colored crayon. Take turns rolling two dice and then add the numbers together. Then find a division problem in the boxes that has that sum for its quotient. The first player to color 3 boxes in a row wins!

$4 \div 2$	$6 \div 2$	$5 \div 1$	$24 \div 2$	$18 \div 2$
$14 \div 2$	$8 \div 4$	$10 \div 2$	$15 \div 5$	$24 \div 4$
$25 \div 5$	$20 \div 5$	$16 \div 4$	$40 \div 4$	$16 \div 4$
$90 \div 10$	$20 \div 5$	$20 \div 4$	$16 \div 2$	$30 \div 5$
$24 \div 4$	$20 \div 2$	$20 \div 10$	$50 \div 5$	$28 \div 4$
$12 \div 2$	$32 \div 4$	$30 \div 10$	$6 \div 1$	$10 \div 1$

Divide by 3 or 6

In this lesson, we will practice dividing by 3 or 6. Dividing by 3 means we split the number into 3 equal groups, so there are 3 in each group. One way we can solve a division problem with 3, or any number, is to draw dots representing the total amount. We then circle groups of 3 to see how many groups we can make.

For example:

$18 \div 3 =$ ____

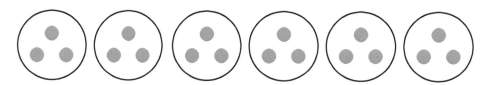

$18 \div 3 = 6$

We could also use repeated subtraction to subtract 3 from 18 and see how many times we need to subtract 3 to get to 0.

$18 - 3 = 15$ $15 - 3 = 12$ $12 - 3 = 9$ $9 - 3 = 6$ $6 - 3 = 3$ $3 - 3 = 0$

We need to subtract 3 from 18 six times to get to 0.

We can use division by 3 to help us divide by 6. We can first divide the whole number by 3, then divide the quotient by 2.

For example, to solve $18 \div 6 =$ ____, we can first divide 18 by 3 to get 6. We then divide 6 by 2 to get 3, so $18 \div 6 = 3$.

PRACTICE EXERCISE 13.1

Directions: Solve the following division facts.

1. $3 \div 3 =$ ____

2. $9 \div 3 =$ ____

3. $6 \div 3 =$ ____

4. $15 \div 3 =$ ____

5. $30 \div 3 =$ ____

6. $24 \div 8 =$ ____

7.   Rylee sold 9 cookies at the school bake fair. There were 3 cookies in each bag. How many bags of cookies did Rylee sell?

8.   A cake recipe needs 3 eggs. How many cakes can be baked with 27 eggs?

PRACTICE EXERCISE 13.2

Directions: Solve the following division facts.

1. $12 \div 6 =$ ____

2. $18 \div 6 =$ ____

3. $6 \div 1 =$ ____

4. $30 \div 6 =$ ____

5. $24 \div 6 =$ ____

6. $48 \div 6 =$ ____

7.   Every 6 minutes, a new car is produced by a car factory. How many cars can be produced in 42 minutes?

8.   There are 6 runners on a relay team. If there are 54 runners in all, how many relay teams are there?

Divide by 7, 8, or 9

In this lesson, we will practice dividing by 7, 8, or 9. To do this, we can use many of the strategies we have already used to multiply or divide other numbers.

For example, if we want to divide 28 by 7, we can draw 28 dots. Then we can circle groups of 7 dots to see how many groups we can make:

$28 \div 7 = 4$

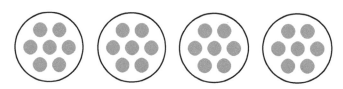

We can also use repeated subtraction to divide. If we want divide 40 by 8, we can subtract 8 from 40 and see how many times we need to subtract 8 to get to 0.

$40 - 8 = 32$ $32 - 8 = 24$ $24 - 8 = 16$ $16 - 8 = 8$ $8 - 8 = 0$

We need to subtract 8 from 40 five times to get to 0, so $40 \div 8 = 5$.

Another strategy we can use to divide is a number line. If we want to solve $63 \div 9$, we can start at 63 on a number line and see how many jumps of 9 we can make to get to 0. As you can see in the picture below, we can make 7 jumps of 9, so $63 \div 9 = 7$.

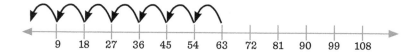

PRACTICE EXERCISE 14.1

Directions: Solve the following division facts.

1. 7 ÷ 7 = ____
2. 21 ÷ 7 = ____
3. 35 ÷ 7 = ____
4. 16 ÷ 8 = ____
5. 48 ÷ 8 = ____
6. 64 ÷ 8 = ____

7. There are 42 T-shirts on display in a store. If each pile has 7 T-shirts, how many piles of T-shirts are there?

8. Paige spent 56 minutes working on homework. She had 8 math problems to solve for homework. If each problem took the same amount of time to solve, how long did Paige spend on each problem?

PRACTICE EXERCISE 14.2

Directions: Solve the following division facts.

1. 9 ÷ 9 = ____
2. 14 ÷ 7 = ____
3. 18 ÷ 9 = ____
4. 24 ÷ 8 = ____
5. 36 ÷ 9 = ____
6. 81 ÷ 9 = ____

7. Ms. Malloy's class grew 54 carrots in the school garden. If the class wanted to use these carrots to make 9 equal batches of vegetable soup, how many carrots would they use in each batch?

8. The chocolate factory made 63 pieces of chocolate fudge. If the factory packages the fudge in boxes, with 9 pieces of fudge in each box, how many boxes will they need?

Relationship Between Multiplication and Division

In this lesson, we will practice solving multiplication and division problems using fact families. A fact family is a group of math facts using the same number. When you learned addition and subtraction, you may have used fact families. For example, with the numbers 2, 3, and 5, we can create four math facts, two for addition and two for subtraction. The facts are $2 + 3 = 5$, $3 + 2 = 5$, $5 - 2 = 3$, and $5 - 3 = 2$.

We can use also use fact families to solve multiplication and division problems. If we have the numbers 3, 6, and 18, we can create four math facts, two for multiplication and two for division. The facts are $3 \times 6 = 18$, $6 \times 3 = 18$, $18 \div 6 = 3$, and $18 \div 3 = 6$.

A fact family can be shown using a triangle where the numbers are connected by multiplication or division. If we want to figure out what 3×6 equals, we know that we have already used 3 and 6, but the number we are missing from the fact family is 18. So we can say that $3 \times 6 = 18$. Because of the commutative property, we can also say that $6 \times 3 = 18$.

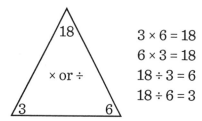

$$3 \times 6 = 18$$
$$6 \times 3 = 18$$
$$18 \div 3 = 6$$
$$18 \div 6 = 3$$

We can use this strategy not only for multiplication but also for division. If we want to know what $18 \div 3$ equals, we can look at the fact family and know that we have already used 18 and 3, but the number missing from the fact family is 6. So we can say $18 \div 3 = 6$. We can also say that $18 \div 6 = 3$.

PRACTICE EXERCISE 15.1

Directions: Use the fact family triangles to solve the following multiplication and division facts.

1.

4 × 5 = _____

5 × 4 = _____

20 ÷ 4 = _____

20 ÷ 5 = _____

2.

5 × 7 = _____

7 × 5 = _____

35 ÷ 5 = _____

35 ÷ 7 = _____

3.

6 × 7 = _____

7 × 6 = _____

42 ÷ 6 = _____

42 ÷ 7 = _____

4.

4 × 9 = _____

9 × 4 = _____

36 ÷ 4 = _____

36 ÷ 9 = _____

5.

6 × 8 = _____

8 × 6 = _____

48 ÷ 6 = _____

48 ÷ 8 = _____

6.

8 × 9 = _____

9 × 8 = _____

72 ÷ 8 = _____

72 ÷ 9 = _____

PRACTICE EXERCISE 15.2

Directions: Find the missing factor for the following.

1. 5 × _____ = 5

2. 3 × _____ = 12

3. 24 ÷ _____ = 6

4. 40 ÷ _____ = 8

5. 6 × _____ = 36

6. 7 × _____ = 42

DIVIDE BY 1 THROUGH 10

Name: _____ Time: _____

Directions: Find the quotient for the following.

1. $\quad$ 4 $\div 4$	2. $\quad$ 6 $\div 3$	3. $\quad$ 7 $\div 1$	4. $\quad$ 18 $\div 3$	5. $\quad$ 8 $\div 4$
6. $\quad$ 10 $\div 5$	7. $\quad$ 45 $\div 5$	8. $\quad$ 36 $\div 4$	9. $\quad$ 32 $\div 4$	10. $\quad$ 30 $\div 5$
11. $\quad$ 50 $\div 10$	12. $\quad$ 36 $\div 4$	13. $\quad$ 18 $\div 6$	14. $\quad$ 14 $\div 7$	15. $\quad$ 36 $\div 6$
16. $\quad$ 9 $\div 9$	17. $\quad$ 42 $\div 6$	18. $\quad$ 28 $\div 7$	19. $\quad$ 49 $\div 7$	20. $\quad$ 10 $\div 5$
21. $\quad$ 63 $\div 7$	22. $\quad$ 80 $\div 8$	23. $\quad$ 32 $\div 8$	24. $\quad$ 48 $\div 8$	25. $\quad$ 16 $\div 2$
26. $\quad$ 36 $\div 9$	27. $\quad$ 70 $\div 7$	28. $\quad$ 72 $\div 8$	29. $\quad$ 64 $\div 8$	30. $\quad$ 81 $\div 9$

MULTIPLICATION AND DIVISION MAZE

Directions: Solve the first equation indicated by "Start," coloring in the squares, including the correct answer. Then solve the next equation along the path immediately following the answer to the equation you just solved. Color in the squares. Repeat until you reach the end.

Start →	4 x 1 =	5	12 ÷ 2 =	14	2 x 9 =	8	12 ÷ 4 =	6
	4		3		7		4 8	
3	10 ÷ 2 =	5	8 x 2 =	4	6 x 2 =	14	24 ÷ 4 =	9
	4 2		16		27		8	
9	64 ÷ 8 =	6	7 x 1 =	7	6 x 8 =	12	8 x 7 =	16
	7		8		4 8		4 5	
10	64 ÷ 8 =	5	9 x 3 =	17	7 x 7 =	49	9 x 2 =	4
	9		2 4		7		18	
14	24 ÷ 8 =	8	1 x 1 =	12	4 x 4 =	4	6 x 6 =	6
	9		6		3		36	
4	36 ÷ 6 =	8	7 x 4 =	21	9 x 3 =	12	81 ÷ 9 =	9

PART 2

GRADE 4

Writing Whole Numbers in Expanded and Written Form

Let's review place value. Place value tells you the value of each digit in a number. In the number 325, the 5 is in the ones place and has a value of 5 ones, or 5. The 2 is in the tens place and has a value of 2 tens, or 20. The 3 is in the hundreds place and has a value of 3 hundreds, or 300. When we write a number in expanded form in a place value chart, we expand it to show the value of each digit.

If we want to write the number 2,857 in expanded form, it could be written in a place value chart to see the place value of each digit.

The value of the 2 is really 2,000, the value of the digit 8 is 800, the value of the digit 5 is 50, and the value of the digit 7 is 7 ones. We use these values to write the expanded form, using addition signs between each value.

Millions	Hundred Thousands	Ten Thousands	Thousands	Hundreds	Tens	Ones

Millions	Hundred Thousands	Ten Thousands	Thousands	Hundreds	Tens	Ones
			2	8	5	7

$(2 \times 1{,}000) + (8 \times 100) + (5 \times 10) + (7 \times 1)$

Sometimes we need to regroup whole numbers. We may need to know how many hundreds are in two thousand: 2,000 is the same as 1,000 × 2. We can use the place value chart to help us do this.

Thousands	Hundreds	Tens	Ones
2	0	0	0
2	0	0	0
2	0	0	0

2,000 = 20 hundreds
2,000 = 200 tens
2,000 = 2,000 ones

PRACTICE EXERCISE 1.1

Directions: Write each number in expanded form.

1. 2,786 _____

2. 7,834 _____

3. 14,329 _____

Directions: Write each number in word form.

4. 3,897 _____

5. 50,810 _____

PRACTICE EXERCISE 1.2

Directions: Regroup the numbers following.

1. How many hundreds are in 8,000? _____

2. How many tens are in 4,000? _____

3. How many thousands are in 30,000? _____

4. What is another way to make 3,600? _____

   a. 3 thousands plus 10 hundreds

   b. 2 thousands plus 16 hundreds

   c. 3 thousands plus 16 tens

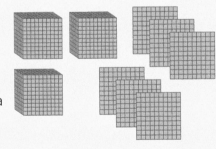

5. Regroup to express the numbers in a different way.

   23,640 = 2 ten thousands + 3 thou-sands + 6 hundreds + 4 tens

   23,640 = 2 ten thousands + 3 thousands + 5 hundreds + ★ tens

   ★ = _____

How 10 Relates to Place Value and Comparing Multi-Digit Numbers

In this lesson, we will practice using place value to help us compare numbers.

Notice that every time we move over one place value to the left, we increase the value by a factor of 10.

We can use a place value chart to help us compare two numbers. Let's say we want to compare 54,545 and 54,455. First, we think about what each digit means.

We see that both numbers have the same value in the ten thousands place and the thousands place value chart. We see that in the hundreds place 54,545 has 5 hundreds and 54,455 has only 4 hundreds. That means 54,545 > 54,455.

We can compare numbers using the greater than, less than, or equal signs.

	$\times 10$	$\times 10$	$\times 10$	$\times 10$	$\times 10$	$\times 10$
Millions	Hundred Thousands	Ten Thousands	Thousands	Hundreds	Tens	Ones

Millions	Hundred Thousands	Ten Thousands	Thousands	Hundreds	Tens	Ones
		5	4	5	4	5

Millions	Hundred Thousands	Ten Thousands	Thousands	Hundreds	Tens	Ones
		5	4	4	5	5

> means **is greater than** (The first number is greater than the second number.)

< means **is less than** (The first number is less than the second number.)

= means **is equal to** (The first number is equal to or the same as the second number.)

PRACTICE EXERCISE 2.1

Directions: Circle the correct answer for each problem.

1. Select the statement that explains the relationship between 40 and 4.

   a. 40 is 10 more than 4.   c. 40 is 10 times greater than 4.

   b. 40 is 10 times less than 4.

2. Which of the following is equal to 6 hundreds × 10?

   a. 6 hundred thousands   c. 6 tens

   b. 6 thousands

3. Select the statement that explains the relationship between 44,000 and 4,400.

   a. 44,000 is 10 times greater   c. 4,400 is 10 more than
      than 4,400.   44,000.

   b. 4,400 is 10 less than 44,000.

4. Start with the number 28. Multiply 28 by 10. The 8 will end up in the _____ place.

   a. ones   c. hundreds

   b. tens

PRACTICE EXERCISE 2.2

Directions: Complete the comparison by choosing >, <, or =. Remember, we can compare numbers using the greater than, less than, or equal signs. (See page opposite.)

1. 7,754 _____ 7,795

2. 5,619 _____ 5,619

3. 844,600 _____ 844,712

4. 644,461 _____ 636,643

Comparing with Multiplication

In this lesson, we will practice comparing using multiplication. In multiplication, we compare two things, or sets, that need to be multiplied. For example, the claw machine on the right, has two times, or twice, as many prizes as the claw machine on the left.

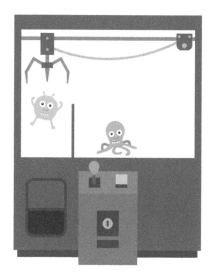 

The claw machine on the left has 2 prizes in it. The machine on the right has 4 prizes because 2 × 2 = 4.

Let's try an example:

Kevin's piece of candy is 4 in. (inches) long. Kelly's piece of candy is 3 times longer than Kevin's piece of candy. How long is Kelly's piece of candy?

Kelly's candy = 3 × 4 in. = 12 in.

Kelly's candy is 12 in. long.

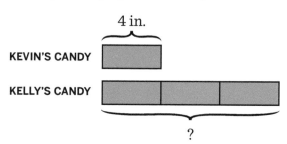

PRACTICE EXERCISE 3.1

Directions: Solve each problem.

1. Which statement represents the equation 4 × 8 = 32?

    a. 32 is 4 more than 8.

    b. 32 is 4 times greater than 8.

    c. 4 is 8 less than 32.

    d. 4 is 8 times greater than 32.

2. Which statement represents the equation 2 × 6 = 12?

    a. 12 times greater than 2 is 6.

    b. 12 is 2 more than 6.

    c. 2 is 6 less than 12.

    d. 12 is 2 times greater than 6.

3. Which statement represents the equation 7 × 9 = 63?

    a. 63 is 7 more than 9.

    b. 7 is 9 less than 63.

    c. 9 is 63 times greater than 7.

    d. 63 is 7 times greater than 9.

4. The number 60 is 6 times greater than 10. Write this comparison as a multiplication equation. _____

PRACTICE EXERCISE 3.2

Directions: Solve each problem.

1. A bicycle is 5 feet long. A bus is 35 feet long. Complete the comparison: The bus is _____ times as long as the bicycle.

2. Lupe has 45 crayons at school. This is 5 times as many crayons as Lupe has at home. Which equation will help us find how many crayons Lupe has at home?

    a. ___ × 45 = 5   b. 5 × 45 = ___   c. 5 × ___ = 45

3. Marco and Mary were collecting seashells. Mary collected 42 seashells, which is 6 times as many seashells as Marco collected. Which equation will help us find how many seashells Marco collected?

    a. 6 × ___ = 42   b. 42 × 6 = ___   c. ___ × 42 = 6

DRILL 1

MULTIPLICATION AND DIVISION FACTS

Name: _____ Time: _____

Directions: Find the product or quotient.

1. $\begin{array}{r} 2 \\ \times 8 \\ \hline \end{array}$	2. $\begin{array}{r} 8 \\ \times 1 \\ \hline \end{array}$	3. $\begin{array}{r} 7 \\ \times 8 \\ \hline \end{array}$	4. $\begin{array}{r} 3 \\ \times 2 \\ \hline \end{array}$	5. $\begin{array}{r} 4 \\ \times 0 \\ \hline \end{array}$
6. $\begin{array}{r} 5 \\ \times 8 \\ \hline \end{array}$	7. $\begin{array}{r} 0 \\ \times 7 \\ \hline \end{array}$	8. $\begin{array}{r} 2 \\ \times 2 \\ \hline \end{array}$	9. $\begin{array}{r} 8 \\ \times 5 \\ \hline \end{array}$	10. $\begin{array}{r} 4 \\ \times 9 \\ \hline \end{array}$
11. $\begin{array}{r} 4 \\ \times 3 \\ \hline \end{array}$	12. $\begin{array}{r} 6 \\ \times 5 \\ \hline \end{array}$	13. $\begin{array}{r} 6 \\ \times 3 \\ \hline \end{array}$	14. $\begin{array}{r} 5 \\ \times 5 \\ \hline \end{array}$	15. $\begin{array}{r} 9 \\ \times 6 \\ \hline \end{array}$
16. $\begin{array}{r} 12 \\ \div 3 \\ \hline \end{array}$	17. $\begin{array}{r} 18 \\ \div 6 \\ \hline \end{array}$	18. $\begin{array}{r} 10 \\ \div 5 \\ \hline \end{array}$	19. $\begin{array}{r} 40 \\ \div 10 \\ \hline \end{array}$	20. $\begin{array}{r} 36 \\ \div 9 \\ \hline \end{array}$
21. $\begin{array}{r} 25 \\ \div 5 \\ \hline \end{array}$	22. $\begin{array}{r} 33 \\ \div 11 \\ \hline \end{array}$	23. $\begin{array}{r} 72 \\ \div 9 \\ \hline \end{array}$	24. $\begin{array}{r} 36 \\ \div 12 \\ \hline \end{array}$	25. $\begin{array}{r} 42 \\ \div 7 \\ \hline \end{array}$
26. $\begin{array}{r} 24 \\ \div 8 \\ \hline \end{array}$	27. $\begin{array}{r} 66 \\ \div 11 \\ \hline \end{array}$	28. $\begin{array}{r} 20 \\ \div 5 \\ \hline \end{array}$	29. $\begin{array}{r} 12 \\ \div 6 \\ \hline \end{array}$	30. $\begin{array}{r} 64 \\ \div 8 \\ \hline \end{array}$

MATH SEARCH

Directions: Find the answers to the clues and color in the answers using the colors in the code.

6	1	2	7	8	0	3	5	5	1
4	9	3	7	1	5	8	2	6	5
3	8	0	8	4	6	4	7	7	0
2	0	6	1	2	6	9	3	2	8
7	1	2	2	3	8	0	1	4	0
1	3	4	0	4	7	1	4	6	9
3	5	6	9	7	5	0	1	2	1
5	7	5	6	4	1	2	3	8	3

red	(4 x 1,000) + (6 x 100) + (7 x 1)	dark blue	8,000 + 30 + 5
orange	Thirty-two thousand and seven hundred and thirteen	tan	70,000 + 5,000 + 10 + 2
yellow	100,000 + 50,000 + 800 + 9	purple	(5 x 100,000) + (6 x 10,000) + (4 x 1,000) + (1 x 100) + (2 x 10) + (3 x 1)
green	(1 x 100) + (2 x 10)	pink	Nine thousand and eight hundred and one
light blue	Twenty-three thousand and sixty-two	brown	(8 x 100) + (1 x 1)

51

Multiplication by 10s, 100s, and 1,000s

If we solve 5×10, we say we have 5 tens, which is 50.

If we solve 5×100, we say we have 5 hundreds, which is 500.

If we solve $5 \times 1,000$, we say we have 5 thousands, which is 5,000.

If you look at these numbers on a place value chart, you'll see that, each time, the digits shift over one place value to the left.

Let's try an example:

$425 \times 10 =$ ____

We say 425 tens. We know we are moving to the tens place, so all of the digits are going to move one place value to the left. The 5 will be in the tens place, the 2 will be in the hundreds place, and the 4 will now be in the thousands place.

Millions	Hundred Thousands	Ten Thousands	Thousands	Hundreds	Tens	Ones
						5
					5	0
				5	0	0
			5	0	0	0

Millions	Hundred Thousands	Ten Thousands	Thousands	Hundreds	Tens	Ones
			4	2	5	0

If we multiply by 100, the digits are going to shift two place values to the left because the hundreds place is two place values from the ones place.

For example:

$331 \times 100 = 33,100$

If we multiply by 1,000, the digits are going to shift three place values to the left because the thousands place is three place values from the ones place.

$514 \times 1,000 = 514,000$

PRACTICE EXERCISE 4.1

Directions: Solve each multiplication problem.

1. $27 \times 10 =$ _____

2. $34 \times 100 =$ _____

3. $57 \times 1{,}000 =$ _____

4. $254 \times 10 =$ _____

5. $317 \times 10 =$ _____

6. $29 \times 100 =$ _____

7. $82 \times 100 =$ _____

8. $93 \times 1{,}000 =$ _____

PRACTICE EXERCISE 4.2

Directions: Complete the following equations.

1. $215 \times$ _____ $= 2{,}150$

2. $34 \times$ _____ $= 3{,}400$

3. $64 \times$ _____ $= 64{,}000$

4. $210 \times$ _____ $= 21{,}000$

5. $544 \times$ _____ $= 5{,}440$

6. $772 \times$ _____ $= 772{,}000$

7. $545 \times$ _____ $= 54{,}500$

8. $31 \times$ _____ $= 310$

Multi-Digit Multiplication and Area Models

In this lesson, we will practice using the area model to help us multiply larger numbers.

345 × 5

First, show the problem as the area of a rectangle.

Next, break the rectangle into smaller areas. You can do this using expanded form: 345 = 300 + 40 + 5.

Then multiply to find the area of each of the smaller rectangles.

Last, we add these products together to find the area of the original rectangle.

1,500 + 200 + 25 = 1,725

345 × 5 = 1,725

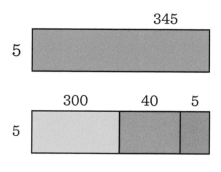

If we want to multiply a two-digit number by a two-digit number we can use the same area model—and break both factors into smaller rectangles. Let's look at multiplying 27 × 32.

First, show the problem as the area of a rectangle.

Next, reconstruct the rectangle. Break apart both factors by using expanded form: 27 = 20 + 7 and 32 = 30 + 2

Then, we multiply to find the area of each of the smaller rectangles.

Last, we add these products to find the area of the original rectangle.

600 + 210 + 40 + 14 = 864

27 × 32 = 864

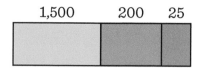

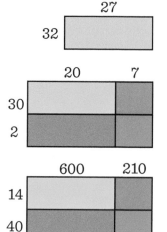

PRACTICE EXERCISE 5.1

Directions: Solve the following multiplication problems.

1. $36 \times 5 = $ _____
2. $32 \times 6 = $ _____
3. $59 \times 8 = $ _____
4. $825 \times 5 = $ _____
5. $348 \times 7 = $ _____
6. $531 \times 8 = $ _____
7. $1{,}847 \times 2 = $ _____
8. $2{,}925 \times 4 = $ _____

PRACTICE EXERCISE 5.2

Directions: Solve each multiplication problem.

1. $12 \times 24 = $ _____
2. $22 \times 31 = $ _____
3. $43 \times 34 = $ _____
4. $53 \times 27 = $ _____
5. $65 \times 38 = $ _____
6. $68 \times 36 = $ _____
7. $72 \times 48 = $ _____
8. $63 \times 84 = $ _____

Estimate Products

In this lesson, we will practice estimating, or finding an approximate value to the exact answer. In other words, we are finding an answer that is close to the actual answer. Estimation is an important skill that can help us determine the reasonableness of our answers. In this lesson, we are going to learn how to estimate the products of two numbers.

Let's try an example:

$42 \times 7 =$ _____

The first thing we will do is round the first number to the nearest place: 42 rounds to 40. The 7 is a one-digit number, so we can keep it as is. We now have 40×7. We multiply these two numbers together to find the estimate: $40 \times 7 = 280$.

We can then say that $42 \times 7 \approx 280$. The squiggly equal sign ($\approx$) shows that this is an estimate, or approximate amount. Instead of "equal to" we say "is about," so 42 times 7 is about 280.

If we were to find the exact answer to 42×7, it would be 294, so we can see that our estimate is close to the exact answer.

Now let's try estimating when we multiply two-digit numbers.

$38 \times 12 =$ _____

This time, we round both numbers because they are both two-digit numbers: 38 rounds to 40 and 12 rounds to 10. We then multiply $40 \times 10 = 400$.

$38 \times 12 \approx 400$

PRACTICE EXERCISE 6.1

Directions: Estimate the product.

1. $36 \times 5 \approx$ _____

2. $32 \times 6 \approx$ _____

3. $59 \times 8 \approx$ _____

4. $825 \times 5 \approx$ _____

5. $348 \times 7 \approx$ _____

6. $531 \times 8 \approx$ _____

7. $1,847 \times 2 \approx$ _____

8. $2,925 \times 4 \approx$ _____

PRACTICE EXERCISE 6.2

Directions: Estimate the product.

1. $23 \times 14 \approx$ _____

2. $36 \times 26 \approx$ _____

3. $41 \times 19 \approx$ _____

4. $54 \times 24 \approx$ _____

5. $65 \times 37 \approx$ _____

6. $77 \times 62 \approx$ _____

7. $71 \times 83 \approx$ _____

8. $85 \times 85 \approx$ _____

MULTIPLICATION AND DIVISION FACTS

Name: _____ Time: _____

Directions: Find the product or quotient.

1. 6 ×9	2. 8 ×1	3. 5 ×5	4. 6 ×8	5. 6 ×3
6. 8 ×7	7. 8 ×8	8. 11 ×4	9. 8 ×5	10. 11 ×11
11. 6 ×4	12. 3 ×7	13. 4 ×10	14. 3 ×12	15. 8 ×8
16. 45 ÷9	17. 60 ÷10	18. 132 ÷11	19. 44 ÷11	20. 72 ÷8
21. 42 ÷6	22. 132 ÷12	23. 70 ÷10	24. 24 ÷12	25. 16 ÷4
26. 80 ÷8	27. 18 ÷3	28. 70 ÷7	29. 24 ÷4	30. 40 ÷8

TILE TIME

Directions: Cut the number tiles from the bottom of the page. Then use those tiles to solve the area model multiplication problems that follow. You will use each digit only once.

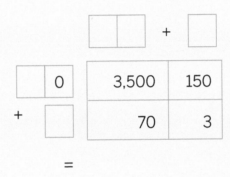

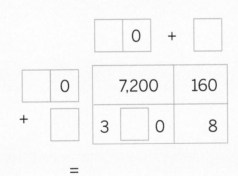

0	1	2	3	4
5	6	7	8	9

Multiply with Partial Products

In this lesson, we will practice using a method called partial products, another way to multiply multi-digit numbers. Similar to the area model, we will use expanded form to help us break the numbers into smaller parts.

Let's try an example:

$538 \times 35 =$ ____

PARTIAL PRODUCT

	Expanded form
538	$(500 + 30 + 8)$
$\times\,35$	$(30 + 5)$

Next, we will use the distributive property, which means you can break apart two factors and then multiply both the addends (the numbers you add together) by the other factor. Then add together the products to come up with the same answer as multiplying the two original factors.

For example, if we try to multiply 12×3:

- We can break up the 12 into $10 + 2$.
- Then multiply $10 \times 3 = 30$ and $2 \times 3 = 6$.
- If we add these two products together, $30 + 6 = 36$, we get the same answer as $12 \times 3 = 36$.

Let's try this with the problem we are working on: $538 \times 35 =$ ____

We take the 5 from 35 and multiply that by the 8, then by the 30, and last by the 500 from 538. After that, we multiply the 30 from 35 by the 8, then by the 30, and last by the 500 from 538. You can see this process in the illustration.

PARTIAL PRODUCT

	Expanded form
538	$(500 + 30 + 8)$
$\times\,35$	$(30 + 5)$
40	5×8
150	5×30
2,500	5×500
240	30×8
900	30×30
15,000	30×500
18,830	

PRACTICE EXERCISE 7.1

Directions: Solve each multiplication problem.

1. $22 \times 5 =$ _____

2. $35 \times 3 =$ _____

3. $28 \times 4 =$ _____

4. $212 \times 4 =$ _____

5. $232 \times 6 =$ _____

6. $623 \times 8 =$ _____

7. $2{,}281 \times 4 =$ _____

8. $5{,}313 \times 5 =$ _____

PRACTICE EXERCISE 7.2

Directions: Solve each multiplication problem.

1. $18 \times 23 =$ _____

2. $24 \times 25 =$ _____

3. $44 \times 22 =$ _____

4. $51 \times 36 =$ _____

5. $61 \times 42 =$ _____

6. $52 \times 35 =$ _____

7. $74 \times 48 =$ _____

8. $86 \times 54 =$ _____

Remainders

In this lesson, we will practice division problems with remainders. Sometimes when we divide a number into equal groups, there are some items left over. These leftover items are called remainders. Let's look at an example of what this means.

$23 \div 3 =$

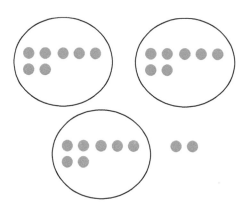

Here we have divided a group of 23 dots into 3 equal groups. Each group has 7 dots. We can see that there are 2 dots left over because we can't divide them equally among the groups. We call these leftovers the remainders. In equation form, we write this as $23 \div 3 = 7$ R. 2.

Let's try another example using repeated subtraction:

Remainder

33, 28, 23, 18, 13, 8, $\boxed{3}$

-5   -5   -5   -5   -5   -5

$33 \div 5 = $ _____

We can see that we were able to subtract 5 from 33 six times and that we have 3 left over as a remainder.

$33 \div 5 = 6$ R. 3

PRACTICE EXERCISE 8.1

Directions: Solve each problem by circling the correct answer or filling in the blank.

1. The number left over at the end of division is called the _____.
   a. quotient
   c. dividend

   b. remainder
   d. divisor

2. Sometimes, we cannot divide a number fully into equal groups.
   a. True
   b. False

3. Find the remainder: $40 \div 6 = 6$ R. _____

4. Find the remainder: $17 \div 2 = 8$ R. _____

5. Find the remainder: $34 \div 4 = 8$ R. _____

6. Find the remainder: $20 \div 8 = 2$ R. _____

7. Find the remainder: $35 \div 8 = 4$ R. _____

8. Find the remainder: $61 \div 9 = 6$ R. _____

PRACTICE EXERCISE 8.2

Directions: Solve each division problem.

1. $14 \div 3 =$ _____
2. $27 \div 4 =$ _____
3. $38 \div 3 =$ _____
4. $57 \div 5 =$ _____

5. $62 \div 6 =$ _____
6. $83 \div 8 =$ _____
7. $89 \div 9 =$ _____
8. $97 \div 10 =$ _____

Divide Multiples of 10, 100, and 1,000

In this lesson, we will practice dividing multiples of 10, 100, and 1,000 using patterns with zeros. Look at the following division problems. Compare the number of zeros in the quotient to the number of zeros in the dividend and divisor. What pattern do you see?

$9,000 \div 3 = 3,000$

$9,000 \div 30 = 300$

$9,000 \div 300 = 30$

$9,000 \div 3,000 = 3$

Notice that the number of zeros in the quotient is equal to the difference in the number of zeros in the dividend and divisor. We can use this pattern when we divide by multiples of 10, 100, and 1,000.

Let's try an example:

$6,000 \div 200 = \underline{\quad\quad}$

First, we use the digits that are *not* zero to make a division problem. In this example, those digits are 6 and 2, so $6 \div 2 = 3$.

Then we look at the remaining zeros and subtract the number of remaining zeros in the divisor from the number of remaining zeros in the dividend. The result tells us how many zeros should be in the quotient.

In the example, we have 3 zeros in 6,000 and 2 zeros in 200. If we subtract the zeros, $3 - 2 = 1$, we know there should be 1 zero in the quotient.

$6,000 \div 200 = 30$

PRACTICE EXERCISE 9.1

Directions: Solve the following division problems.

1. 160 ÷ 4 = _____
2. 180 ÷ 6 = _____
3. 240 ÷ 3 = _____
4. 280 ÷ 7 = _____
5. 2,400 ÷ 6 = _____
6. 4,000 ÷ 8 = _____
7. 3,200 ÷ 8 = _____
8. 2,700 ÷ 9 = _____

PRACTICE EXERCISE 9.2

Directions: Solve the following division problems.

1. 200 ÷ 50 = _____
2. 180 ÷ 30 = _____
3. 900 ÷ 30 = _____
4. 400 ÷ 80 = _____
5. 8,000 ÷ 400 = _____
6. 9,000 ÷ 30 = _____
7. 6,000 ÷ 200 = _____
8. 6,000 ÷ 300 = _____

MULTIPLICATION AND DIVISION FACTS

Name: _____ Time: _____

Directions: Find the product or quotient.

1. 3 ×3	2. 12 ×10	3. 5 ×4	4. 5 ×7	5. 5 ×6
6. 12 ×4	7. 9 ×8	8. 8 ×8	9. 10 ×3	10. 11 ×11
11. 7 ×4	12. 9 ×7	13. 4 ×12	14. 5 ×12	15. 7 ×9
16. 40 ÷8	17. 120 ÷10	18. 33 ÷11	19. 84 ÷12	20. 20 ÷4
21. 30 ÷6	22. 132 ÷12	23. 80 ÷10	24. 36 ÷12	25. 24 ÷6
26. 30 ÷3	27. 40 ÷8	28. 99 ÷9	29. 44 ÷11	30. 132 ÷11

MYSTERY PICTURE

FUN WITH MATH 3

Directions: Solve each problem and record the answer. Color the answers according to the key to reveal the mystery picture.

Yellow	Blue	Black
1,400 ÷ 7 = _____	2,800 ÷ 40 = _____	1,600 ÷ 10 = _____
1,600 ÷ 80 = _____	1,500 ÷ 5 = _____	6,000 ÷ 600 = _____
1,500 ÷ 30 = _____	4,500 ÷ 50 = _____	3,600 ÷ 90 = _____
4,000 ÷ 40 = _____		
2,100 ÷ 10 = _____		
5,400 ÷ 90 = _____		

70	300	90	70	90	300	90	70	300	90	70	70	300	90	70
300	90	70	90	300	200	20	50	100	210	300	90	70	300	90
70	300	90	60	200	20	50	100	210	60	50	20	90	70	300
90	300	200	20	50	100	210	60	200	20	50	100	210	90	70
70	90	60	210	100	50	20	200	60	210	100	50	20	300	90
300	200	20	50	100	160	210	60	210	10	200	20	50	100	70
90	210	60	200	20	40	50	100	60	160	210	200	20	50	300
70	200	20	50	100	210	60	200	50	50	20	100	210	60	70
300	60	210	100	160	50	20	200	60	210	10	60	200	20	90
90	200	20	50	100	40	210	60	200	160	200	20	50	100	300
90	70	200	20	50	100	160	10	40	200	20	50	100	70	300
70	300	20	50	100	210	60	200	20	50	100	210	60	90	70
90	300	70	200	20	50	100	210	60	200	20	50	70	300	90
70	300	90	70	300	200	20	50	100	210	70	300	90	70	300
90	70	300	90	70	70	300	90	70	300	300	70	90	90	70

Division with Place Value

Let's try an example: $725 \div 6 =$ ___

Draw a rectangle to represent the place values that are in the dividend and the divisor. Write the numbers as shown.

Then ask, "How many 6 hundreds can be divided into 725?" We can make one group. Put 100 in the hundreds column and multiply 100 by 6 to make 600, which we write underneath the 725 in the hundreds column. We subtract 600 from 725.

Take the 125 and bring it to the tens place. Repeat the process, asking, "How many groups of 6 tens can be divided into 125?" We can make two groups. Two groups of 10 is 20. Put 20 in the tens column and multiply 20 by 6 to make 120. Write this underneath 125. Then, subtract 120 from 125.

Take the 5 and bring it to the ones column. Repeat the process. We can't make any groups of 6 ones. Put 0 in the ones place and multiply 0 by 6. $6 \times 0 = 0$. Write 0 underneath the 5 in the ones place and subtract. We have a remainder of 5. Add the numbers under the hundreds, tens, and ones columns ($100 + 20 + 0 = 120$) to determine the quotient.

$725 \div 6 = 120$ R. 5

DIVIDEND
725

hundreds	tens	ones
725		

DIVISOR 6

DIVIDEND
725

hundreds	tens	ones
100		
725		
-600		
125		

DIVISOR 6

DIVIDEND
725

hundreds	tens	ones
100	20	
725	125	
-600	-120	
125	5	

DIVISOR 6

DIVIDEND
725

hundreds	tens	ones
100	20	0
725	125	5
-600	-120	-0
125	5	5

DIVISOR 6

PRACTICE EXERCISE 10.1

Directions: Solve each division problem.

1. 852 ÷ 2 = _____

   Dividend
   ____

hundreds	tens	ones

   Divisor ____

2. 504 ÷ 4 = _____

   Dividend
   ____

hundreds	tens	ones

   Divisor ____

3. 615 ÷ 5 = _____

   Dividend
   ____

hundreds	tens	ones

   Divisor ____

4. 624 ÷ 4 = _____

   Dividend
   ____

hundreds	tens	ones

   Divisor ____

PRACTICE EXERCISE 10.2

Directions: Solve each division problem.

1. 656 ÷ 3 = _____

   Dividend
   ____

hundreds	tens	ones

   Divisor ____

2. 951 ÷ 5 = _____

   Dividend
   ____

hundreds	tens	ones

   Divisor ____

3. 698 ÷ 6 = _____

   Dividend
   ____

hundreds	tens	ones

   Divisor ____

4. 862 ÷ 4 = _____

   Dividend
   ____

hundreds	tens	ones

   Divisor ____

Division with Area Models

Let's try an example:

$168 \div 4 =$ ___

We are going to break down the dividend until we get to zero. We can do that with the multiplication facts that we know, using the factor of 4 (because the divisor is 4) to chip away at the dividend.

Let's start with 25. There are 4 quarters in 1 dollar, and a quarter is worth 25 cents, so we can see that $4 \times 25 = 100$. We write 25 on the top of the rectangle and separate the rectangle to show that area. Next, multiply $25 \times 4 = 100$. Take that product and subtract it from the dividend.

Do we know any math facts involving the factor of 4 that would get us close to 68? One choice is the tens facts. We place a 10 on the top of the rectangle and separate the rectangle to show that area. Next, we multiply $10 \times 4 = 40$. Take that product and subtract it from the dividend.

Do we know any math facts with a factor of 4 and a product of 28? We know that $7 \times 4 = 28$. We then take that product and subtract.

The last step is to add the numbers at the top of our rectangle to find our quotient: $25 + 10 + 7 = 42$.

$168 \div 4 = 42$

```
             168

 4 [      ]
```

```
     25          168
   ┌─────┬────┐  −100
 4 │ 100 │    │   68
   └─────┴────┘
```

```
     25    10       168
   ┌─────┬────┬──┐  −100
 4 │ 100 │ 40 │  │   68
   └─────┴────┴──┘   −40
                      28
```

```
     25    10   7    168
   ┌─────┬────┬────┐ −100
 4 │ 100 │ 40 │ 28 │   68
   └─────┴────┴────┘  −40
                       28
                      −28
                        0
```

PRACTICE EXERCISE 11.1

Directions: Solve each division problem.

1. $32 \div 2 =$	2. $72 \div 4 =$
3. $225 \div 5 =$	4. $186 \div 6 =$
5. $189 \div 9 =$	6. $672 \div 7 =$

PRACTICE EXERCISE 11.2

Directions: Solve the following word problems.

1. At a baseball game, the snack shack sold 280 bags of popcorn in 4 hours. How many bags of popcorn did they sell each hour?

2. Ramona sold 360 boxes of Girl Scout cookies in 6 weeks. How many boxes did she sell each week?

3. Mr. Korf bought 4 new pencil boxes. He has 260 pencils. He wants to put the pencils in the boxes so each box has the same number of pencils. How many pencils will there be in each box?

4. A school received a shipment of 984 books. If there are 6 fourth-grade classrooms, how many books will each classroom get?

Estimate Quotients

In this lesson, we will practice estimating the quotient of two numbers. Similar to what we did when estimating products with multiplication, we find an approximate value to the exact answer when estimating to find a division quotient.

Let's try an example:

$162 \div 4 = \underline{\hspace{2em}}$

The first thing we will do is round the first number in the problem to the greatest place: 162 rounds to 160. The 4 is a one-digit number, so we can keep it as is. We now have $160 \div 4$. We divide 160 into 4 equal groups to find the estimate: $160 \div 4 = 40$.

We can then say that $160 \div 4 \approx 40$. Remember from our estimating products lesson that the squiggly equal sign ($\approx$) shows this is an estimate, or approximate amount. Instead of "is equal to," we say "is about," so 162 divided by 4 is about 40. The exact answer to $162 \div 4$ is 40 R. 2, so the estimate is close to the exact answer.

Sometimes we may not want to round to the greatest place if the division is easier to do by rounding to a different place.

For example:

$3,635 \div 6 = \underline{\hspace{2em}}$

If we rounded 3,635 to the greatest place, it would be 4,000, which is not easily divisible by 6. Instead, we could round 3,635 to the hundreds place, which is 3,600. This division problem is much easier:
$3,600 \div 6 = 600$.

Now let's try estimating when we divide by two-digit numbers.

$178 \div 24 = \underline{\hspace{2em}}$

This time we round both numbers because they are both multi-digit numbers: 178 rounds to 180, and 24 rounds to 20. We divide 180 into 20 equal groups to find the estimate: $180 \div 20 = 9$.

$180 \div 20 \approx 9$

PRACTICE EXERCISE 12.1

Directions: Estimate the quotient.

1. $308 \div 3 \approx$ _____

2. $271 \div 9 \approx$ _____

3. $283 \div 4 \approx$ _____

4. $397 \div 4 \approx$ _____

5. $279 \div 7 \approx$ _____

6. $993 \div 2 \approx$ _____

7. $321 \div 8 \approx$ _____

8. $897 \div 9 \approx$ _____

PRACTICE EXERCISE 12.2

Directions: Estimate the quotient.

1. $2{,}003 \div 5 \approx$ _____

2. $2{,}435 \div 3 \approx$ _____

3. $2{,}807 \div 4 \approx$ _____

4. $2{,}789 \div 7 \approx$ _____

5. $3{,}517 \div 7 \approx$ _____

6. $5{,}457 \div 6 \approx$ _____

7. $6{,}334 \div 7 \approx$ _____

8. $5{,}437 \div 9 \approx$ _____

MULTIPLICATION AND DIVISION

Name: _____ Time: _____

Directions: Find the product or quotient.

1. 3 ×10	2. 30 ×10	3. 50 ×4	4. 60 ×7	5. 100 ×5
6. 12 ×8	7. 90 ×8	8. 100 ×8	9. 11 ×10	10. 20 ×20
11. 80 ×50	12. 90 ×70	13. 40 ×50	14. 4 ×20	15. 80 ×60
16. 400 ÷5	17. 110 ÷10	18. 300 ÷30	19. 80 ÷40	20. 200 ÷40
21. 300 ÷60	22. 120 ÷40	23. 800 ÷10	24. 360 ÷9	25. 240 ÷6
26. 240 ÷3	27. 560 ÷8	28. 540 ÷9	29. 440 ÷10	30. 640 ÷8

SPIN A QUOTIENT

Directions: Use a paper clip and pencil to make a spinner. Spin the paper clip and find a division number sentence with a quotient that matches the number you landed on. Color in that box. Try to color in 3 boxes in a row.

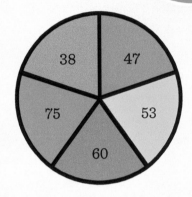

180 ÷ 3 = _____	190 ÷ 5 = _____	375 ÷ 5 = _____	240 ÷ 4 = _____	376 ÷ 8 = _____
152 ÷ 4 = _____	235 ÷ 5 = _____	318 ÷ 6 = _____	300 ÷ 5 = _____	150 ÷ 2 = _____
76 ÷ 2 = _____	450 ÷ 6 = _____	60 ÷ 1 = _____	424 ÷ 8 = _____	329 ÷ 7 = _____
360 ÷ 6 = _____	228 ÷ 6 = _____	525 ÷ 7 = _____	212 ÷ 4 = _____	188 ÷ 4 = _____
114 ÷ 3 = _____	282 ÷ 6 = _____	342 ÷ 9 = _____	420 ÷ 7 = _____	600 ÷ 8 = _____

13

Multi-Digit Division with Partial Quotients

Let's practice solving division problems using partial quotients.

Here's an example:

3,240 ÷ 20 = ____

When using partial quotients, we set the problem up like this:

$$20 \overline{)\ 3,240}$$

We need to subtract a multiple of 20 that is less than 3,240. An easy one to subtract is 100 groups of 20, which is 2,000.

$$
\begin{array}{r}
20 \overline{)\ 3,240} \\
-2,000 \quad \times 100 \\
\hline
-1,240
\end{array}
$$

Now we need to subtract a multiple of 20 that is less than 1,240 as we get closer to zero. We can use 60 groups of 20, which gives us 1,200.

$$
\begin{array}{r}
20 \overline{)\ 3,240} \\
-2,000 \quad \times 100 \\
\hline
-1,240 \\
-1,200 \quad \times 60 \\
\hline
40
\end{array}
$$

We see that we have 40 left. We can multiply 2 groups of 20 to get 40.

$$
\begin{array}{r}
20 \overline{)\ 3,240} \\
-2,000 \quad \times 100 \\
\hline
-1,240 \\
-1,200 \quad \times 60 \\
\hline
40 \\
-40 \quad \times 2
\end{array}
$$

Last, we add the numbers to the right that we used to multiply to find the quotient: 100 + 60 + 2 = 162.

3,240 ÷ 20 = 162

PRACTICE EXERCISE 13.1

Directions: Use the partial quotients method to solve the following division problems.

1. 22) 418	2. 24) 768
3. 38) 1,216	4. 42) 1,470

PRACTICE EXERCISE 13.2

Directions: Use the partial quotients method to solve the following division problems.

1. 24) 500	2. 32) 1,250
3. 40) 3,750	4. 52) 4,470

14

Multiplication and Division Word Problems

In this lesson, you can put your skills to work solving word problems. There are many strategies for doing this. Here are some tips!

Ask yourself:

"What question is the problem asking?"

"What information do I need to solve the problem?"

"Is there any information given that I don't need?" If so, cross it out!

"Can I draw pictures or a model to solve the problem?"

"Is my answer reasonable?"

Let's try an example:

A teacher is ordering T-shirts for the class field trip. Each T-shirt costs $18. The teacher needs 24 shirts. How much will they cost?

First, ask, "What question is the problem asking?" The problem is asking how much 24 T-shirts will cost. If you were to model the problem, it might look like this:

$$
\begin{array}{c}
\ \ \ \ 24 \\
18 \ \boxed{}
\end{array}
$$

Based on this model, you may decide to use the area model to solve it. First, break down each of the factors into expanded form.

	20	4
10	200	40
8	160	32

Then multiply each of the factors. Last, add all the products: 200 + 160 + 40 + 32 = 432. The T-shirts will cost $432.

PRACTICE EXERCISE 14.1

Directions: Solve the following word problems.

1. Each school bus has 24 seats. There are 12 school buses. How many seats are there among all the school buses?

2. There are 24 hours in 1 day. How many hours are there in 2 weeks?

3. Tyler has 15 piles of Halloween candy. Each pile has 25 pieces of candy in it. How many pieces of candy does Tyler have in all?

4. Cody is having a pizza party. There will be 12 people at the party. Each person will eat 2 pieces of pizza. Which size pizza does Cody need to order?

   a. Small,
      12 slices
   b. Medium,
      20 slices
   c. Large,
      30 slices

5. Isabella and Javier have a lemonade stand. They sell each cup of lemonade for 25 cents. If they sell 18 cups, how much money will they make?

PRACTICE EXERCISE 14.2

Directions: Solve the following word problems.

1. Dwight has 78 football cards. He wants to give half of the cards to his brother. How many cards will Dwight have left?

2. The elementary school is hosting a barbecue. They need 176 hot dog buns. Hot dog buns come in packages of 8. How many packages of hot dog buns does the school need to buy?

3. The cafeteria tables each seat 12 students. There are 252 students in the cafeteria. How many tables are there?

4. Rylee loves solving math problems! Her math book has 375 problems to solve. If Rylee solves 25 problems each day, how many days will it take her to finish the problems?

5. A bakery received a shipment of 313 eggs. If it takes 3 eggs to make each cake, how many cakes can they make?

Multi-Step Word Problems

In this lesson, we will practice solving multi-step word problems, which are word problems with more than one step. There may be two steps using the same operation, such as two multiplication problems, or there may be two different operations, such as multiplication and then addition.

We use a process for multi-step word problems that is similar to the way we solved word problems previously, but this time we will identify each step of the problem first.

Let's try an example: Miles bought 16 books at the book fair for $4 each. He gave the cashier $100. How much change did Miles receive?

First we ask, "What question is the problem asking?" The problem is asking how much change Miles got back after he paid for the books.

We need to know how much money Miles spent. That is the first step in this multi-step problem. We can find out how much Miles spent by multiplying $4 by 16, so 16 × 4 = 64. Miles spent $64.

Step 1	Step 2
16	100
×4	−64
$64	$36

The second step is to subtract the $64 Miles spent from the $100 he used to pay for the books: $100 – 64 = $36. Miles received $36 in change.

PRACTICE EXERCISE 15.1

Directions: Solve the following word problems.

1. A baker was preparing cookies and brownies for the bake shop. The baker baked 3 trays of cookies that each held 10 cookies and the baker baked 20 brownies. How many sweet treats did the baker bake in all?

2. Six cookie sheets have 4 rows of cookies each. There are 3 cookies in each row. How many cookies are there total?

3. One fish tank at a pet store has 12 fish in it. A larger tank has 4 times as many fish. How many fish are in both tanks?

4. Lucy and Colby were writing mystery numbers. Lucy's number had 23 tens and 18 ones. Colby's number had 2 hundreds, 4 tens, and 6 ones. Who wrote the number with the greatest value?

PRACTICE EXERCISE 15.2

Directions: Solve the following word problems.

1. Stephanie and her mom were at the grocery store looking at boxes of chips for Stephanie's lunch. The smaller box had 24 bags of chips and the larger box had 29 bags of chips. Stephanie thought they would get more chips if they bought 6 of the smaller boxes. Her mom thought they would get more chips if they bought 4 of the larger boxes. Who is correct?

2. A teacher was putting together school supplies for her students. The teacher had 24 boxes, and put 12 pencils and 14 markers in each box. How many supplies did the teacher put in all of the boxes together?

3. Kayla went school shopping and bought 7 pairs of jeans for $15 each and 9 shirts for $8 each. How much did Kayla spend in all?

4. A family of 5 went to the amusement park. The tickets to get into the park were $14 each. They also purchased a food package for each person that cost $11 each. How much did they spend?

MULTIPLICATION AND DIVISION

Name: _____ Time: _____

Directions: Find the product or quotient.

1. $\begin{array}{r} 6 \\ \times 20 \\ \hline \end{array}$	2. $\begin{array}{r} 9 \\ \times 30 \\ \hline \end{array}$	3. $\begin{array}{r} 600 \\ \times 2 \\ \hline \end{array}$	4. $\begin{array}{r} 30 \\ \times 70 \\ \hline \end{array}$	5. $\begin{array}{r} 10 \\ \times 50 \\ \hline \end{array}$
6. $\begin{array}{r} 120 \\ \times 10 \\ \hline \end{array}$	7. $\begin{array}{r} 30 \\ \times 80 \\ \hline \end{array}$	8. $\begin{array}{r} 100 \\ \times 22 \\ \hline \end{array}$	9. $\begin{array}{r} 56 \\ \times 10 \\ \hline \end{array}$	10. $\begin{array}{r} 27 \\ \times 10 \\ \hline \end{array}$
11. $\begin{array}{r} 90 \\ \times 60 \\ \hline \end{array}$	12. $\begin{array}{r} 80 \\ \times 80 \\ \hline \end{array}$	13. $\begin{array}{r} 60 \\ \times 70 \\ \hline \end{array}$	14. $\begin{array}{r} 4 \\ \times 200 \\ \hline \end{array}$	15. $\begin{array}{r} 90 \\ \times 90 \\ \hline \end{array}$
16. $\begin{array}{r} 600 \\ \div 2 \\ \hline \end{array}$	17. $\begin{array}{r} 9,000 \\ \div 3 \\ \hline \end{array}$	18. $\begin{array}{r} 1,500 \\ \div 5 \\ \hline \end{array}$	19. $\begin{array}{r} 450 \\ \div 50 \\ \hline \end{array}$	20. $\begin{array}{r} 1,200 \\ \div 40 \\ \hline \end{array}$
21. $\begin{array}{r} 300 \\ \div 50 \\ \hline \end{array}$	22. $\begin{array}{r} 3,000 \\ \div 5 \\ \hline \end{array}$	23. $\begin{array}{r} 160 \\ \div 4 \\ \hline \end{array}$	24. $\begin{array}{r} 1,800 \\ \div 6 \\ \hline \end{array}$	25. $\begin{array}{r} 4,800 \\ \div 8 \\ \hline \end{array}$
26. $\begin{array}{r} 6,300 \\ \div 9 \\ \hline \end{array}$	27. $\begin{array}{r} 7,200 \\ \div 90 \\ \hline \end{array}$	28. $\begin{array}{r} 5,600 \\ \div 80 \\ \hline \end{array}$	29. $\begin{array}{r} 810 \\ \div 9 \\ \hline \end{array}$	30. $\begin{array}{r} 5,400 \\ \div 60 \\ \hline \end{array}$

ROLL AND ANSWER

Directions: Roll a pair of dice. Answer the question that corresponds with the sum that you rolled. Look for the quotient in the tic-tac-toe board below. Color it in. Try to color 3 boxes in a row.

2	$2,500 \div 25 =$
3	$3,732 \div 4 =$
4	$1,440 \div 36 =$
5	$7,236 \div 9 =$
6	$300 \div 25 =$
7	$1,440 \div 32 =$
8	$630 \div 6 =$
9	$3,200 \div 100 =$
10	$29,000 \div 100 =$
11	$1,586 \div 13 =$
12	$1,700 \div 25 =$

12	32	40	32
45	68	100	40
105	122	290	122
804	933	12	68

PART 3

GRADE 5

Multiply Three- and Four-Digit Numbers by Two-Digit Numbers

In previous lessons, we learned a variety of strategies to multiply two factors. In this lesson, we are going to learn another strategy to multiply by two factors.

Let's multiply 352 × 67. Line up the problem as shown below.

352
×67

We are going to multiply each digit of the top number by the number in the ones place in the bottom number. We start with the ones place, then the tens place, and finally the hundreds place.

First, we multiply 2 × 7, which is 14. We put the 4 in the ones place and, just as we do with addition, we put the 1 in the tens place from the number 14 on top of the number in the tens place in the top number (the 5 in 352).

Next, we multiply the tens place by 7, so 5 × 7 = 35. We have the 1 we wrote on top that we add to the product, so 35 + 1 = 36. We write the 6 in the tens place and the 3 in the hundreds place in the top number (the 3 in 352).

Then we multiply the hundreds place by 7, so 3 × 7 = 21. We have the 3 we wrote on top that we add to the product, 21 + 3 = 24. Because we don't have any other numbers, we just write the 4 in the hundreds place on the bottom and the 2 next to it in the thousands place.

Next, we repeat this process by multiplying each digit of the top number by the tens place in the bottom number (6). We place a 0 in the ones place as a placeholder first.

```
      3 1
      3 1
     352
   ×  67
   2,464
 +21,120
  23,584
```

Multiply by the number in ones place.
Put a zero below in the ones place.
Multiply by the number in the tens place.
Add them up.

PRACTICE EXERCISE 1.1

Directions: Solve the following problems.

1.
$$431 \times 12$$

2.
$$815 \times 24$$

3.
$$783 \times 42$$

4.
$$725 \times 53$$

5.
$$648 \times 64$$

6.
$$764 \times 78$$

7. There are 209 boxes of soda in a store display. If each box contains 12 cans of soda, how many cans of soda are there in all?

8. Courtney saves $242 a month. How much will she have saved in 21 months?

PRACTICE EXERCISE 1.2

Directions: Solve the following problems.

1.
$$4,310 \times 42$$

2.
$$2,075 \times 33$$

3.
$$4,004 \times 42$$

4.
$$2,803 \times 57$$

5.
$$8,198 \times 62$$

6.
$$5,529 \times 87$$

7. A bird flies 3,831 miles a month. How far does the bird fly in one year?

8. A school is buying a magazine subscription for each student. Each subscription costs $19. If there are 1,089 students, how much will the total cost be?

Multiply Three- and Four-Digit Numbers by Three-Digit Numbers

In this lesson, we will use the same method to multiply by three-digit numbers.

Let's try an example: **2,813 × 416 =** _____

First, we multiply 3 × 6, which is 18. We put the 8 in the ones place and, just as we do with addition, we put the 1 from the number 18 on top of the number in the tens place in the top number (the 1 in 2,813).

Multiply the tens place by 6, so 1 × 6 = 6. We have the 1 we wrote on top that we add to the product, so 6 + 1 = 7. We write the 7 in the tens place.

Then we multiply the hundreds place by 6, so 8 × 6 = 48. We write the 8 in hundreds place and put the 4 on top of the thousands place in the top number (the 8 in 2,813).

Now we multiply the thousands place by 6, so 2 × 6 = 12. We have the 4 on top of the thousands place that we need to add to the product, 12 + 4 = 16. Because we don't have any other numbers, we just write the 6 in the thousands place on the bottom and the 1 next to it in the ten thousands place.

Repeat this process by multiplying each digit of the top number by the tens place in the bottom number (1). Use a 0 as a placeholder in the ones place first.

Again, multiply each digit of the top number by the hundreds place in the bottom number (1). Put a 0 in the ones place and another 0 in the tens place as placeholders.

```
      3  1
      4  1
  2,813
×   416
   1 1
 16,878
 28,130
+1,125,200
1,170,208
```

Multiply by the number in ones place.

Put a zero below in the ones place.

Multiply by the number in the tens place.

Put two zeros below in the ones and tens place.

Multiply by the number in the hundreds place.

Add them up.

PRACTICE EXERCISE 2.1

Directions: Solve the following problems.

1.
442
× 122

2.
213
× 324

3.
481
× 302

4.
346
× 207

5.
662
× 372

6.
746
× 297

7. A publisher prints 512 copies of a book in each print run. If they print 105 runs, how many books will be printed in total?

8. A school purchased 415 new laptops for their students. Each laptop cost $399. What was the total cost of the laptops?

PRACTICE EXERCISE 2.2

Directions: Solve the following problems.

1.
3,051
× 222

2.
4,401
× 305

3.
2,481
× 350

4.
1,346
× 297

5.
8,401
× 372

6.
7,502
× 656

7. An elephant eats 250 pounds of plants in a day. How many pounds of plants would an elephant eat in one year?

8. A furniture store sold 362 televisions last year. If each television cost $549, how much money did the store make?

Multiply Multi-Digit Numbers and Assess the Reasonableness of the Product Using Estimation

When we multiply multi-digit numbers, we may want to check the reasonableness of the product by estimating, which is a good way to check the answers for accuracy. In this lesson, we will practice estimating the product by rounding both factors or by finding compatible numbers for both factors that are easier to multiply.

Let's try an example:

$413 \times 236 = $ _____

To estimate this problem, we are going to round both factors: 413 rounds to 400 and 236 rounds to 200. Then we multiply the rounded numbers, $400 \times 200 = 80,000$. If we solve the actual problem, $413 \times 236 = 97,468$, we can see that our estimate is reasonable.

Let's try another example:

$3,499 \times 102 = $ _____

For this problem, we can find compatible numbers that are easier to multiply and will give us an answer that is closer to the actual answer: 3,499 is close to 3,500 and 102 is close to 100. We will multiply $3,500 \times 100 = 350,000$. If we solve the actual problem, $3,499 \times 102 = 356,898$, we can see that our estimate is reasonable.

PRACTICE EXERCISE 3.1

Directions: Estimate the product first. Solve by using the standard procedure. Use your estimate to check the reasonableness of the product.

Example: 224 × 311

Estimate	Actual
200 × 300 60,000	224 × 311 69,664

2. 729 × 552

Estimate	Actual

1. 552 × 345

Estimate	Actual

3. 778 × 687

Estimate	Actual

PRACTICE EXERCISE 3.2

Directions: Repeat the instructions from the previous exercise.

1. 3,502 × 145

Estimate	Actual

3. 4,753 × 475

Estimate	Actual

2. 4,320 × 342

Estimate	Actual

4. 5,075 × 486

Estimate	Actual

MULTIPLICATION AND DIVISION FACTS

Name: _____ Time: _____

Directions: Find the product or quotient.

1. $\begin{array}{r} 2 \\ \times 10 \\ \hline \end{array}$	2. $\begin{array}{r} 12 \\ \times 10 \\ \hline \end{array}$	3. $\begin{array}{r} 12 \\ \times 100 \\ \hline \end{array}$	4. $\begin{array}{r} 5 \\ \times 10 \\ \hline \end{array}$	5. $\begin{array}{r} 35 \\ \times 10 \\ \hline \end{array}$
6. $\begin{array}{r} 35 \\ \times 100 \\ \hline \end{array}$	7. $\begin{array}{r} 10 \\ \times 7 \\ \hline \end{array}$	8. $\begin{array}{r} 27 \\ \times 10 \\ \hline \end{array}$	9. $\begin{array}{r} 27 \\ \times 100 \\ \hline \end{array}$	10. $\begin{array}{r} 8 \\ \times 2 \\ \hline \end{array}$
11. $\begin{array}{r} 8 \\ \times 20 \\ \hline \end{array}$	12. $\begin{array}{r} 16 \\ \times 10 \\ \hline \end{array}$	13. $\begin{array}{r} 16 \\ \times 2 \\ \hline \end{array}$	14. $\begin{array}{r} 16 \\ \times 20 \\ \hline \end{array}$	15. $\begin{array}{r} 33 \\ \times 2 \\ \hline \end{array}$
16. $\begin{array}{r} 8 \\ \div 4 \\ \hline \end{array}$	17. $\begin{array}{r} 88 \\ \div 4 \\ \hline \end{array}$	18. $\begin{array}{r} 8,800 \\ \div 400 \\ \hline \end{array}$	19. $\begin{array}{r} 240 \\ \div 10 \\ \hline \end{array}$	20. $\begin{array}{r} 480 \\ \div 20 \\ \hline \end{array}$
21. $\begin{array}{r} 2,400 \\ \div 100 \\ \hline \end{array}$	22. $\begin{array}{r} 82 \\ \div 2 \\ \hline \end{array}$	23. $\begin{array}{r} 820 \\ \div 20 \\ \hline \end{array}$	24. $\begin{array}{r} 24 \\ \div 2 \\ \hline \end{array}$	25. $\begin{array}{r} 36 \\ \div 3 \\ \hline \end{array}$
26. $\begin{array}{r} 360 \\ \div 30 \\ \hline \end{array}$	27. $\begin{array}{r} 3,600 \\ \div 300 \\ \hline \end{array}$	28. $\begin{array}{r} 45 \\ \div 3 \\ \hline \end{array}$	29. $\begin{array}{r} 450 \\ \div 30 \\ \hline \end{array}$	30. $\begin{array}{r} 4,500 \\ \div 300 \\ \hline \end{array}$

WEIRD AND RANDOM FACT

FUN WITH MATH 1

Directions: Answer the following questions. Use the answers to fill in the correct letters and solve the weird and random fact. Some letters may be used more than once.

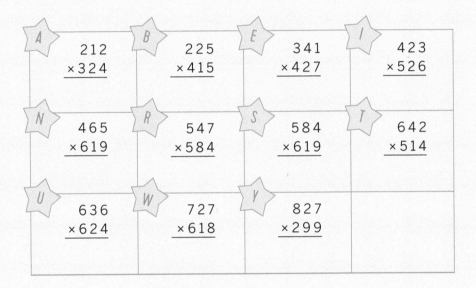

A	B	E	I
212 × 324	225 × 415	341 × 427	423 × 526
N 465 × 619	**R** 547 × 584	**S** 584 × 619	**T** 642 × 514
U 636 × 624	**W** 727 × 618	**Y** 827 × 299	

___
68,688

___ ___ ___ ___ ___ ___ ___ ___ ___ ___
361,496 329,988 319,446 68,688 449,286 93,375 145,607 319,448 319,448 247,273

,

___ ___ ___ ___ ___
222,498 361,496 287,835 329,988 68,688

___ ___ ___ ___ ___**,** ___ ___ ___ ___
93,375 145,607 319,448 319,448 247,273 93,375 396,864 329,988 68,688

___ ___ ___ ___ ___ ___ ___ ___**!**
93,375 68,688 287,835 68,688 287,835 68,688 222,498 361,496

93

Multiplying and Dividing Whole Numbers by 10, 100, and 1,000

Let's start with the number 3,500 written in a place value chart.

If you are multiplying or dividing by 10, the digits move one place because there is one 0 in 10. If you are multiplying or dividing by 100, the digits move two places because there are two 00s in 100. If you are multiplying or dividing by 1,000, the digits move three places.

Millions	Hundred Thousands	Ten Thousands	Thousands	Hundreds	Tens	Ones
			3	5	0	0

10	digits move	1 place
100	digits move	2 places
1,000	digits move	3 places

When we **multiply** the numbers, *the digits move to the left*, and we add that number of zeros to the place values that have been left empty.

× digits move **to the left** ⟵
÷ digits move **to the right** ⟶

When we **divide** the numbers, *the digits move to the right*, and we remove that number of zeros.

The place value chart below shows how the digits move based on the number they are multiplied or divided by.

	Millions	Hundred Thousands	Ten Thousands	Thousands	Hundreds	Tens	Ones	Tenths	Hundredths	Thousandths
× 10			3	5	0	0	0			
× 100		3	5	0	0	0	0			
× 1000	3	5	0	0	0	0	0			
÷ 10					3	5	0			
÷ 100						3	5			
÷ 1000							3	5		

PRACTICE EXERCISE 4.1

Directions: Solve the following problems.

1. $410 \times 10 = $ _____

2. $410 \times 100 = $ _____

3. $5,000 \times 1,000 = $ _____

4. $207 \times 10 = $ _____

5. $207 \times 1,000 = $ _____

6. $990 \times 10 = $ _____

7. $990 \times 100 = $ _____

8. $990 \times 1,000 = $ _____

PRACTICE EXERCISE 4.2

Directions: Solve the following problems.

1. $4,000 \div 10 = $ _____

2. $4,000 \div 100 = $ _____

3. $4,000 \div 1,000 = $ _____

4. $990 \div 10 = $ _____

5. $990 \div 100 = $ _____

6. $990 \div 1,000 = $ _____

7. $575 \div 100 = $ _____

8. $818 \div 1,000 = $ _____

Divide Three-Digit Dividends by Two-Digit Divisors

In this lesson, we will practice how to divide three-digit numbers by two-digit numbers.

Let's try an example:

790 ÷ 18 = _____

First, we think about place value. In the number 790, we have 7 hundreds, so we ask, "Can we divide 7 hundreds by 18?" Since we need to regroup to do this, we will work with 79 tens and see if we can divide that by 18. We can first make an estimate by rounding: $79 \approx 80$ and $18 \approx 20$, so $80 \div 20 = 4$. We record the 4 tens in the tens place (above the 9).

We multiply $18 \times 4 = 72$ and write that product underneath 79, then subtract to find the remainder. We now have 70 ones. We ask, "How many groups of 18 can we make from 70?" We can estimate by using compatible numbers of 60 for 70 and 20 for 18, so $60 \div 20 = 3$. We record the 3 ones in the ones place (above the 0).

We then multiply $18 \times 3 = 54$ and write that product under 70, then subtract to find the remainder. When we subtract 70 – 54, we have 16 left over. We can't make a group of 18 with 16, so that is the remainder:
790 ÷ 18 = 43 R. 16.

Estimates	Solution	Check	
80 tens ÷ 20 = 4 tens 60 tens ÷ 20 = 3 ones	43 18 ⟌ 790 -72 70 -54 16	2 43 × 18 344 +430 774	774 + 16 790

PRACTICE EXERCISE 5.1

Directions: Divide to solve the following problems.

1. 830 ÷ 42 =

Estimate	Solution	Check

3. 643 ÷ 32 =

Estimate	Solution	Check

2. 840 ÷ 38 =

Estimate	Solution	Check

4. 804 ÷ 56 =

Estimate	Solution	Check

PRACTICE EXERCISE 5.2

Directions: Divide to solve the following problems.

1. 419 ÷ 13 =

Estimate	Solution	Check

3. 387 ÷ 12 =

Estimate	Solution	Check

2. 608 ÷ 47 =

Estimate	Solution	Check

4. 585 ÷ 14 =

Estimate	Solution	Check

Divide Four-Digit Dividends by Two-Digit and Three-Digit Divisors

In this lesson, we will practice using the partial quotients division method to divide four-digit numbers.

Let's try an example:

$1{,}950 \div 12 =$ ____

```
12 | 1,950
```

Remember, when we use the partial quotients method, we set up the problem like this:

Then we need to subtract a multiple of 12 that is less than 1,950. An easy one to subtract is 100 groups of 12, which is 1,200.

```
12 | 1,950
     -1,200  × 100
        750
```

Next, we need to subtract a multiple of 12 that is less than 750 as we get closer to zero. We can use 10 groups of 12, which gives us 120.

Then we need to subtract a multiple of 12 that is less than 630 as we get closer to zero. Since we know that 12 × 5 = 60, we can use that fact to help us see that 12 × 50 = 600. For the next factors, we can use 50 groups of 12, which gives us 600.

```
12 | 1,950
     -1,200  × 100
        750
       -120  × 10
        630
```

Now we need to subtract a multiple of 12 that is less than 30 as we get closer to zero. We can use 2 groups of 12, which gives us 24.

We are left with 6, so we do not have enough to make a group of 12. This will be the remainder.

```
12 | 1,950
     -1,200  × 100
        750
       -120  × 10
        630
       -600  × 50
         30
```

Last, we add up the numbers to the right that we used to multiply to find the quotient:
$100 + 10 + 50 + 2 = 162$.

$1{,}950 \div 12 = 162$ R. 6

```
12 | 1,950
     -1,200  × 100
        750
       -120  × 10
        630
       -600  × 50
         30
        -24  × 2
          6
```

PRACTICE EXERCISE 6.1

Directions: Find the quotients.

1. 3,859 ÷ 23 = _____

2. 3,536 ÷ 52 = _____

3. 3,165 ÷ 55 = _____

4. 7,242 ÷ 24 = _____

5. 3,424 ÷ 63 = _____

6. 9,152 ÷ 49 = _____

7. A store is celebrating its 29th year of being in business by giving a prize to every 29th customer. The store had 7,281 customers this year. How many prizes did they give away?

8. A flower shop received a shipment of 1,064 flowers. They put the flowers into vases with 24 flowers in each. They used the flowers that were left over to decorate the shop. How many flowers did they use to decorate the shop?

PRACTICE EXERCISE 6.2

Directions: Find the quotients.

1. 4,859 ÷ 323 = _____

2. 4,368 ÷ 152 = _____

3. 5,385 ÷ 555 = _____

4. 6,649 ÷ 631 = _____

5. 7,647 ÷ 613 = _____

6. 9,247 ÷ 308 = _____

7. A store earned $4,500 selling bicycles that cost $125 each. How many bicycles did they sell?

8. A school is selling cookie dough for a fundraiser. They need to sell at least 8,000 containers of cookie dough. If there are 626 students at the school, how many containers does each student need to sell?

MULTIPLICATION AND DIVISION FACTS

Name: _____ Time: _____

Directions: Find the product or quotient.

1. _____ x 78 = 780	2. _____ x 78 = 7,800	3. 553 x _____ = 5,530	4. 1,000 x _____ = 6,000	5. _____ x 10 = 8,800
6. 100 x _____ = 5,100	7. _____ x 23 = 230	8. _____ x 23 = 2,300	9. _____ x 46 = 460	10. _____ x 46 = 46,000
11. 10 x _____ = 640	12. _____ x 100 = 7,800	13. 1,000 x 8 = _____	14. _____ x 64 = 640	15. _____ x 64 = 64,000
16. 271 ÷ 10	17. 271 ÷ 100	18. 899 ÷ 10	19. 899 ÷ 100	20. 2,700 ÷ 10
21. 2,700 ÷ 100	22. 2,700 ÷ 1,000	23. 990 ÷ 100	24. 262 ÷ 10	25. 195 ÷ 100
26. 360 ÷ 10	27. 3,600 ÷ 1,000	28. 390 ÷ 10	29. 390 ÷ 100	30. 3,900 ÷ 1,000

MATH SEARCH

Directions: Solve each problem. After you have solved the problem, find and circle the answer in the puzzle. Answers can be found going forward, down, and diagonally.

3	1	2	4	7	5	0	4	7	6
9	1	7	0	3	9	3	0	1	9
5	3	9	0	8	1	5	2	3	1
7	6	1	3	3	7	8	2	3	0
1	4	5	3	9	6	1	5	6	3
2	2	6	7	5	2	3	1	6	4

$355 \div 5 =$ _____

$920 \div 4 =$ _____

$2,184 \div 6 =$ _____

$7,414 \div 22 =$ _____

$5,616 \div 27 =$ _____

$1,116 \div 9 =$ _____

$1,700 \div 10 =$ _____

$5,250 \div 7 =$ _____

$1,156 \div 34 =$ _____

Divide Multi-Digit Numbers by One- and Two-Digit Divisors and Assess the Reasonableness of the Quotient

Just as we did with multiplication, when we divide multi-digit numbers, we may want to check the reasonableness of our quotient by estimating. This is a good way to check the answers for accuracy. In this lesson, we will practice estimating by rounding both the dividend and the divisor, or by finding compatible numbers for both that are easier to divide.

Let's try an example:

$894 \div 288 =$ _____

To estimate this problem, we are going to round both the dividend and the divisor: 894 rounds to 900 and 288 rounds to 300. Then we divide the rounded numbers: $900 \div 300 = 3$. If we solve the actual problem, $894 \div 288 = 3$ R. 30, we can see that our estimate is reasonable.

Let's try another example:

$1{,}204 \div 7 =$ _____

For this problem, we can find compatible numbers that are easier to divide and will give us an answer that is close to the actual answer. We know that 1,204 is close to 1,400. We will keep the divisor 7, because it is easy to divide 1,400 by 7. We will divide $1{,}400 \div 7 = 200$. If we solve the actual problem $1{,}204 \div 7 = 172$, we can see that our estimate is reasonable.

PRACTICE EXERCISE 7.1

Directions: Estimate the quotient by rounding, then solve the actual problem. Use your estimate to check if the product is reasonable.

1. 6,839 ÷ 7

Estimate	Actual

3. 4,955 ÷ 5

Estimate	Actual

2. 7,848 ÷ 8

Estimate	Actual

4. 5,236 ÷ 2

Estimate	Actual

PRACTICE EXER.CISE 7.2

Directions: Estimate the quotient using compatible numbers. Then solve the actual problem. Use your estimate to check if the product is reasonable.

1. 4,540 ÷ 5

Estimate	Actual

3. 3,495 ÷ 5

Estimate	Actual

2. 6,544 ÷ 8

Estimate	Actual

4. 3,615 ÷ 5

Estimate	Actual

Multiply a One-Digit Whole Number by a Decimal

In this lesson, we will practice multiplying a one-digit whole number by a decimal. When we multiply a whole number by a decimal, it is similar to multiplying two whole numbers.

Let's try an example:

$3 \times 0.4 = \underline{\quad}$

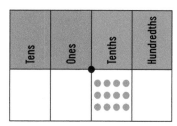

Just as we did when we multiplied whole numbers, we make groups. We have 3 groups of 4 tenths, which is 12 tenths.

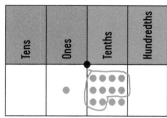

We can regroup 10 of these tenths to make one whole.

Now we have 1 in the ones place and 2 left in the tenths place, or 1.2.

We can also solve this by multiplying the numbers without the decimals ($3 \times 4 = 12$). We then place the decimal back into the answer by seeing how many digits were to the right of the decimal. In the problem, 3×0.4, there is 1 digit (4) to the right of the decimal. The answer needs to have 1 digit to the right of the decimal, so we will place the decimal between the 1 and the 2 in the product. The answer is 1.2.

PRACTICE EXERCISE 8.1

Directions: Find the product.

1. 2 × 0.2 = _____

2. 4 × 0.5 = _____

3. 7 × 0.3 = _____

4. 8 × 0.6 = _____

5. 8 × 0.8 = _____

6. 9 × 0.7 = _____

7. Amy bought 5 oranges that each weighed 0.3 pounds. How much did all the oranges weigh together?

8. Marco's mom is making a salad and she sent Marco to the store to buy some vegetables. Marco bought 3 tomatoes that cost $0.60 each and 2 cucumbers that cost $0.50 each. How much did Marco spend for all the vegetables?

PRACTICE EXERCISE 8.2

Directions: Find the product.

1. 2 × 2.4 = _____

2. 5 × 5.5 = _____

3. 6 × 4.25 = _____

4. 8 × 1.2 = _____

5. 7 × 6.3 = _____

6. 9 × 4.09 = _____

7. Rylan bought 4 apples that each weighed 0.33 pounds. How much did all the apples weigh together?

8. Mrs. Patel is buying markers for her classroom. Each package of markers costs $2.47. If she buys 8 packages, how much will Mrs. Patel spend?

Multiply a Multi-Digit Whole Number by a Decimal

In this lesson, we will practice multiplying a multi-digit whole number by a decimal. For this activity, we use the same process we did when we multiplied a one-digit whole number by a decimal. We will use the following steps:

1. Remove the decimal.

2. Multiply.

3. Put the decimal back in place based on how many numbers were to the right of the decimal in the original problem.

   Let's try an example:

$23 \times 0.18 =$ _____

First, we remove the decimal and rewrite the problem.

$$\begin{array}{r} 23 \\ \times\,18 \\ \hline \end{array}$$

Next, we multiply as we would whole numbers.

$$\begin{array}{r} {\scriptstyle 2} \\ 23 \\ \times\,18 \\ \hline {\scriptstyle 1} \\ 184 \\ +230 \\ \hline 414 \end{array}$$

Last, we place the decimal point in the product. To do this, we count the number of digits to the right of the decimal in the factors: 0.18 has 2 digits to the right of the decimal point, so we will move the decimal point 2 digits to the left in the product.

$23 \times 0.18 = 4.14$

PRACTICE EXERCISE 9.1

Directions: Find the product.

1. 22 × 0.3 = _____

2. 44 × 0.4 = _____

3. 71 × 0.6 = _____

4. 334 × 0.2 = _____

5. 814 × 0.2 = _____

6. 749 × 0.9 = _____

7. Brian multiplied 28 × 0.3 and got 84. Is he correct? If not, what is the correct answer?

8. Mr. Korf bought packages of crayons for his class. The crayon packages cost $0.75 each. He has 24 students in his class. How much did Mr. Korf spend?

PRACTICE EXERCISE 9.2

Directions: Find the product.

1. 55 × 2.2 = _____

2. 36 × 1.25 = _____

3. 47 × 1.33 = _____

4. 58 × 0.64 = _____

5. 78 × 4.82 = _____

6. 88 × 3.75 = _____

7. Jessica's family is adding tile pavers to their backyard. They bought square tiles that are each 18.4 inches long. If they buy 24 tiles, what length of the backyard will the tiles cover?

8. A school is building a new playground structure that will measure 6.4 meters by 21 meters. What is the area of the playground structure?

MULTIPLYING ONE-DIGIT WHOLE NUMBERS BY DECIMALS

Name: _____ Time: _____

Directions: Find the product.

1. $\begin{array}{r} 1.3 \\ \times\ 3 \\ \hline \end{array}$	2. $\begin{array}{r} 5.1 \\ \times\ 9 \\ \hline \end{array}$	3. $\begin{array}{r} 1.5 \\ \times\ 4 \\ \hline \end{array}$	4. $\begin{array}{r} 8.4 \\ \times\ 2 \\ \hline \end{array}$	5. $\begin{array}{r} 5.4 \\ \times\ 4 \\ \hline \end{array}$
6. $\begin{array}{r} 8.1 \\ \times\ 6 \\ \hline \end{array}$	7. $\begin{array}{r} 7.4 \\ \times\ 2 \\ \hline \end{array}$	8. $\begin{array}{r} 5.0 \\ \times\ 4 \\ \hline \end{array}$	9. $\begin{array}{r} 8.1 \\ \times\ 8 \\ \hline \end{array}$	10. $\begin{array}{r} 6.1 \\ \times\ 5 \\ \hline \end{array}$
11. $\begin{array}{r} 8.1 \\ \times\ 2 \\ \hline \end{array}$	12. $\begin{array}{r} 3.1 \\ \times\ 2 \\ \hline \end{array}$	13. $\begin{array}{r} 3.1 \\ \times\ 3 \\ \hline \end{array}$	14. $\begin{array}{r} 2.1 \\ \times\ 6 \\ \hline \end{array}$	15. $\begin{array}{r} 9.0 \\ \times\ 8 \\ \hline \end{array}$
16. $\begin{array}{r} 1.8 \\ \times\ 7 \\ \hline \end{array}$	17. $\begin{array}{r} 3.3 \\ \times\ 2 \\ \hline \end{array}$	18. $\begin{array}{r} 9.1 \\ \times\ 7 \\ \hline \end{array}$	19. $\begin{array}{r} 1.9 \\ \times\ 3 \\ \hline \end{array}$	20. $\begin{array}{r} 9.4 \\ \times\ 5 \\ \hline \end{array}$
21. $\begin{array}{r} 9.1 \\ \times\ 8 \\ \hline \end{array}$	22. $\begin{array}{r} 5.2 \\ \times\ 3 \\ \hline \end{array}$	23. $\begin{array}{r} 9.4 \\ \times\ 3 \\ \hline \end{array}$	24. $\begin{array}{r} 3.1 \\ \times\ 7 \\ \hline \end{array}$	25. $\begin{array}{r} 4.0 \\ \times\ 2 \\ \hline \end{array}$
26. $\begin{array}{r} 9.1 \\ \times\ 2 \\ \hline \end{array}$	27. $\begin{array}{r} 6.4 \\ \times\ 5 \\ \hline \end{array}$	28. $\begin{array}{r} 8.5 \\ \times\ 3 \\ \hline \end{array}$	29. $\begin{array}{r} 3.1 \\ \times\ 6 \\ \hline \end{array}$	30. $\begin{array}{r} 5.2 \\ \times\ 3 \\ \hline \end{array}$

TRUE OR FALSE CHALLENGE

Directions: Cut out the following problem cards. Choose one of the cards and decide if the answer given to the problem is true or false. Then glue the card to the correct category.

$6.5 \times 10 = 0.65$

$42 \times 0.5 = 2.1$

$1.2 \times 1,000 = 1,200$

$33 \times 0.3 = 9.9$

$5.6 \times 10 = 56$

$48 \times 0.8 = 384$

True

False

Multiply a Decimal by a Decimal

In this lesson, we will practice multiplying a decimal by a decimal. When we multiply a decimal by a decimal, we use the same process that we used when multiplying a whole number by a decimal. We will perform the following steps:

1. Remove the decimals in both factors.

2. Multiply.

3. Count the total number of decimal places *in both factors*. Move the decimal point the same number of places to the left for each decimal place you counted.

   Let's try an example:

$0.6 \times 0.8 =$ _____

First, we remove the decimals and rewrite the problem.

$$\begin{array}{r} 6 \\ \times\, 8 \\ \hline \end{array}$$

Next, we multiply as we would whole numbers: $6 \times 8 = 48$.

If we count the number of digits after the decimal in each factor, we see that we have one digit after the decimal in 0.6 and one digit after the decimal in 0.8 for a total of 2 digits. When we put the decimal back into the product, we move it to the left two places, which gives us 0.48.

$0.6 \times 0.8 = 0.48$

PRACTICE EXERCISE 10.1

Directions: Find the product.

1. 0.4 × 0.2 = _____

2. 0.7 × 0.2 = _____

3. 0.4 × 0.9 = _____

4. 0.7 × 0.6 = _____

5. 0.6 × 0.3 = _____

6. 0.5 × 0.6 = _____

7. Mikaela is in a running club and ran 0.5 miles every day last week. How many miles did Mikaela run in all?

8. A square toy has a length of 3.4 inches. What is the area of the toy? (Remember to use the XX^2 notation in your answer because the area is measured in square units.)

PRACTICE EXERCISE 10.2

Directions: Find the product.

1. 1.2 × 2.2 = _____

2. 2.6 × 3.2 = _____

3. 2.7 × 3.25 = _____

4. 4.01 × 5.3 = _____

5. 4.5 × 4.63 = _____

6. 9.4 × 7.75 = _____

7. One side of a square park is 35.2 yards. What is the area of the park? (Remember to use the XX^2 notation in your answer because the area is measured in square units.)

8. Austin is helping his mom build a flower bed. It is 2.5 yards long and 1.3 yards wide. What is the area of the flower bed? (Remember to use the XX^2 notation in your answer because the area is measured in square units.)

Divide a Decimal by a One-Digit Whole Number

In this lesson, instead of multiplying, we will practice dividing a decimal by a one-digit whole number. Dividing with decimals is just like dividing with whole numbers, with one small difference: the decimal point! Let's try an example to see how it works:

$3.65 \div 5 =$ _____

First, set up your division problem the way you normally set up a long-division problem.

Then put the decimal point in the quotient space right above the decimal in your dividend.

$$5 \overline{)\ 3.65}$$

Put the decimal point right above the other one.

Last, divide as you normally do.

$$
\begin{array}{r}
.73 \\
5 \overline{)\ 3.65} \\
\underline{-3\,5} \\
15 \\
\underline{-15} \\
0
\end{array}
$$

$3.65 \div 5 = .73$

PRACTICE EXERCISE 11.1

Directions: Find the quotient.

1. $2\overline{)24.2}$

2. $4\overline{)0.96}$

3. $2\overline{)4.68}$

4. $6\overline{)46.8}$

5. $7\overline{)14.7}$

6. $3\overline{)96.6}$

7. Two friends went out to lunch. The bill was $25.50, and they split it evenly. How much did each friend pay?

8. Mariah wants to buy a video game that costs $50.00. She decides to save her money for 4 weeks to buy it. If she saves the same amount each week, how much does Mariah need to save?

PRACTICE EXERCISE 11.2

Directions: Find the quotient.

1. $2\overline{)5.8}$

2. $4\overline{)4.8}$

3. $6\overline{)24.6}$

4. $6\overline{)2.88}$

5. $5\overline{)7.25}$

6. $4\overline{)3.76}$

7. Dylan has 5 chores to complete each week. If his allowance is $4.60, how much does Dylan get paid per chore?

8. In science class, Mrs. Geil has 30.6 liters of water for a science experiment. She needs to divide the water equally into 9 containers for a class assignment. How much water will each container have?

Divide a Decimal by a Two-Digit Whole Number

In this lesson, we will practice dividing a decimal by a two-digit whole number. This works exactly the same as dividing a decimal by a one-digit number.

Let's try an example:

$80.3 \div 22 =$ ____

First, set up the division problem the way you normally set up a long-division problem.

Then put the decimal point in the quotient space right above the decimal that is in the dividend.

$$22 \overline{)\ 80.3} \quad \longleftarrow \quad \text{Put the decimal point right above the other one.}$$

Last, divide as you normally do.

$$
\begin{array}{r}
3.65 \\
22 \overline{)\ 80.3} \\
\underline{-66} \\
143 \\
\underline{-132} \\
110 \quad \longleftarrow \quad \text{Add a zero to continue dividing.} \\
\underline{-110} \\
0
\end{array}
$$

Notice that we added a zero after the 11, so we can continue dividing. When we divide with decimals, we don't have remainders; instead, we continue adding zeros to continue dividing.

$80.3 \div 22 = 3.65$

PRACTICE EXERCISE 12.1

Directions: Find the quotient.

1. $10\overline{)24.5}$

2. $14\overline{)32.48}$

3. $12\overline{)8.58}$

4. $26\overline{)75.66}$

5. $23\overline{)338.56}$

6. $16\overline{)171.6}$

7. Baylor bought 10 baseballs that weighed a total of 1,417.4 grams. How much does one baseball weigh?

8. Mariah bought a package of 44 chocolate chip cookies. The total weight of the package of cookies was 39.6 ounces. How much did each cookie weigh?

PRACTICE EXERCISE 12.2

Directions: Find the quotient.

1. $10\overline{)19.8}$

2. $20\overline{)77.1}$

3. $25\overline{)33.5}$

4. $84\overline{)6.72}$

5. $35\overline{)4.9}$

6. $48\overline{)0.36}$

7. A new neighborhood is being built. There are 43.8 acres of land that will be divided into 30 lots. How many acres will each lot contain?

8. A factory used 26.8 kilograms of tomatoes to make 16 jars of spaghetti sauce. How many kilograms of tomatoes did they use for each jar of spaghetti sauce?

DIVIDING DECIMALS BY WHOLE NUMBERS

Name: _____ Time: _____

Directions: Find the quotient.

1. 2.4 ÷ 2	2. 5.6 ÷ 8	3. 8.2 ÷ 2	4. 9.3 ÷ 3	5. 2.4 ÷ 4
6. 3.6 ÷ 6	7. 8.1 ÷ 9	8. 4.2 ÷ 7	9. 2.4 ÷ 6	10. 7.0 ÷ 10
11. 8.1 ÷ 1	12. 4.0 ÷ 8	13. 1.2 ÷ 2	14. 1.5 ÷ 5	15. 4.5 ÷ 5
16. 1.8 ÷ 3	17. 3.2 ÷ 4	18. 0.3 ÷ 10	19. 3.5 ÷ 7	20. 4.9 ÷ 7
21. 3.2 ÷ 8	22. 1.6 ÷ 8	23. 0.32 ÷ 8	24. 3.2 ÷ 1	25. 0.33 ÷ 11
26. 4.5 ÷ 9	27. 6.4 ÷ 2	28. 1.5 ÷ 3	29. 3.5 ÷ 5	30. 1.8 ÷ 6

DECIMAL FUN

Directions: Complete each decimal division problem. Write the letter that matches each solution in the boxes below.

1. 0.84 ÷ 4 =	2. 0.24 ÷ 4 =	3. 47.7 ÷ 6 =
F	J	L
4. 4.7 ÷ 2 =	5. 0.50 ÷ 5 =	6. 0.68 ÷ 4 =
H	E	Y
7. 0.96 ÷ 4 =	8. 0.54 ÷ 6 =	
I	S	

What does a shark like to eat with peanut butter?

0.04	0.10	7.95	7.95	0.017	0.21	0.24	0.09	2.35

Divide a Whole Number by 1 Tenth or 1 Hundredth

In this lesson, we will practice dividing a whole number by 1 tenth or 1 hundredth. When we divide a whole number or a decimal by 1 tenth or 1 hundredth, there are two ways we can solve the problem.

Let's try an example:

$3 \div 0.10 =$ _____

One way that we can solve this problem is to think of everything in terms of tenths. We ask, "How many tenths is equal to 3 wholes?" One whole is equal to 10 tenths, so 3 is equal to 30 tenths.

We could then rewrite the equation as: 30 tenths $\div$ 1 tenth = 30.

We could also rewrite the decimal as a fraction: $3 \div \frac{1}{10} =$ _____.

Dividing by 1 tenth is the same as multiplying by 10, so $3 \times 10 = 30$.

$3 \div 0.10 = 30$

We can do the same thing when we divide a whole number by 1 hundredth: $5 \div 0.01 =$ _____.

We can solve this by thinking of everything in terms of hundredths. We ask, "How many hundredths is equal to 5 wholes?" One whole is equal to 100 hundredths, so 5 is equal to 500 hundredths.

We could then rewrite the equation as 500 hundredths $\div$ 1 hundredth = 500.

We could also rewrite the decimal as a fraction: $5 \div \frac{1}{100} =$ _____.

Dividing by a hundredth is the same as multiplying by 100, so $5 \times 100 = 500$.

PRACTICE EXERCISE 13.1

Directions: Find the quotient.

1. $1 \div 0.01 =$ _____

2. $2 \div 0.01 =$ _____

3. $3 \div 0.01 =$ _____

4. $5 \div 0.01 =$ _____

5. $7 \div 0.01 =$ _____

6. $8 \div 0.01 =$ _____

PRACTICE EXERCISE 13.2

Directions: Find the quotient.

1. $2 \div 0.10 =$ _____

2. $4 \div 0.10 =$ _____

3. $6 \div 0.10 =$ _____

4. $7 \div 0.10 =$ _____

5. $1 \div 0.10 =$ _____

6. $9 \div 0.10 =$ _____

Divide a Whole Number or a Decimal by a Decimal

In this lesson, we will practice how to divide whole numbers and decimals by a decimal.

Let's try an example:

$115 \div 0.5 =$ ____

First, we need to make the decimal a whole number by shifting the decimal over one place to the right. What we do to the divisor, we also need to do to the dividend. So we need to move the decimal place over one place to the right in the dividend, too. We place a 0 in the place before the decimal.

Shift the decimal place over one place value to make a whole number.

Shift the decimal place over the same number of places as you moved in the divisor.

Now we divide as we normally do.

```
        230
0.5 ) 1150
     -10
      15
     -15
      00
```

$115 \div 0.5 = 230$

PRACTICE EXERCISE 14.1

Directions: Find the quotient.

1. $0.4\overline{)33}$

2. $0.5\overline{)97}$

3. $0.8\overline{)368}$

4. $0.8\overline{)11}$

5. $0.04\overline{)565}$

6. $0.05\overline{)72}$

PRACTICE EXERCISE 14.2

Directions: Find the quotient.

1. $0.05\overline{)74}$

2. $0.04\overline{)302}$

3. $0.03\overline{)873}$

4. $0.06\overline{)570}$

5. $0.8\overline{)778}$

6. $0.06\overline{)20}$

Comparing Decimal Place Values

What is the relationship between the 5 in the hundreds place and the 5 in the hundredths place?

2,534.851

- As we move to the right, each place represents $\frac{1}{10}$, or 1 tenth, of the place before it. We can divide by 10 as we move to the right.
- As we move to the left, each place represents 10 times the place before it. We can multiply by 10 as we move to the left.

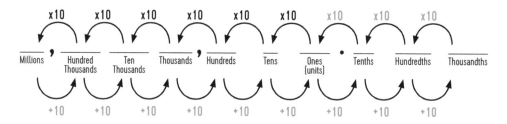

The first 5 is in the hundreds place, 5 × 100, or 5 hundreds (500). The second 5 is in the hundredths place, 5 × 0.01, or 5 hundredths (0.05).

Millions	Hundred Thousands	Ten Thousands	Thousands	Hundreds	Tens	Ones	Tenths	Hundredths	Thousandths
			2	5	3	4	8	5	1

How much do we need to multiply 0.05 (the smaller number) to get 500 (the larger number)? In this case, it is 4 place values, so we need to multiply by 10 four times (10 × 10 × 10 × 10 = 10,000). The first 5 represents 10,000 times the value of the second 5.

PRACTICE EXERCISE 15.1

Directions: Fill in the blanks with the correct answers.

1. The value of the 1 in 1,342 is _____ times the value of the 1 in 42,192.

2. The value of the 8 in 548 is _____ times the value of the 8 in 2,980.7.

3. The value of the 9 in 13.98 is _____ times the value of the 8 in 2,980.7.

4. In which number does the digit 7 have a value that is 0.1 times as great as the digit 7 in 3.876?

   a. 0.705   b. 0.107   c. 27.062   d. 2,976

5. In which number does the digit 6 have a value that is 10 times as great as the digit 6 in 62,405?

   a. 46,707   b. 924,694   c. 37,367   d. 620,288

PRACTICE EXERCISE 15.2

Directions: Fill in the blanks with the correct answers.

1. The value of the 6 in 4.601 is _____ times the value of the 6 in 95.96.

2. The value of the 2 in 342 is _____ times the value of the 2 in 7,326.64.

3. The value of the 2 in 43,290 is _____ times the value of the 2 in 32,165.

4. In which number does the digit 7 have a value that is 10 times as great as the digit 7 in 0.975?

   a. 8.457   b. 7.99   c. 0.73   d. 676.9

5. In which number does the digit 3 have a value that is 10 times as great as the digit 3 in 46.312?

   a. 8.553   b. 3.8553   c. 83.5   d. 508.3

MULTIPLYING AND DIVIDING
ONE-DIGIT WHOLE NUMBERS BY DECIMALS

Name: _____ Time: _____

Directions: Find the product or quotient.

1. 2.3 × 2	2. 0.6 × 4	3. 0.08 × 0.02	4. 0.3 × 9	5. 0.05 × 0.03
6. 0.6 × 6	7. 0.04 × 0.02	8. 0.07 × 0.09	9. 2.1 × 4	10. 0.9 × 6
11. 0.07 × 0.07	12. 0.4 × 8	13. 0.05 × 0.05	14. 1 × 0.025	15. 0.3 × 0.6
16. 2.4 ÷ 3	17. 3.2 ÷ 8	18. 0.8 ÷ 10	19. 3.5 ÷ 5	20. 4.2 ÷ 7
21. 6.4 ÷ 8	22. 1.6 ÷ 4	23. 3.3 ÷ 11	24. 4.5 ÷ 9	25. 0.27 ÷ 3
26. 0.7 ÷ 10	27. 4.2 ÷ 2	28. 4.5 ÷ 5	29. 0.5 ÷ 10	30. 1.8 ÷ 1

SUDOKU

Directions: Fill in each blank with the correct number to solve the problem. Every row, column, and 2 × 2 box ⊞ should contain each of these digits: 1, 2, 3, 4.

3.1 × 0.5 ___5.5	0.6 × 2 1.___	2.2 × 2 4.___	0.7 × 0.9 0.6___
0.8 ⟌ 2.4	0.8 ⟌ 3.2	2.5 ⟌ 5	6.3 ⟌ 6.3
0.7 × 0.6 0.___2	3 × 0.5 ___.5	6 × 0.6 ___.6	0.4 × 0.6 0.___4
3.2 ⟌ 6.4	1.3 ⟌ 3.9	0.7 ⟌ 0.7	0.9 ⟌ 0.36

ANSWER KEY

PART 1: GRADE 3

PRACTICE EXERCISE 1.1

1. 2 groups of 2
   $2 + 2 = 4$
   $2 \times 2 = 4$
2. 2 groups of 3
   $3 + 3 = 6$
   $2 \times 3 = 6$
3. 2 groups of 5
   $5 + 5 = 10$
   $2 \times 5 = 10$
4. 3 groups of 3
   $3 + 3 + 3 = 9$
   $3 \times 3 = 9$
5. 3 groups of 4
   $4 + 4 + 4 = 12$
   $3 \times 4 = 12$
6. 4 groups of 4
   $4 + 4 + 4 + 4 = 16$
   $4 \times 4 = 16$

PRACTICE EXERCISE 1.2

1. $6 + 6 = 12$
2. $3 + 3 + 3 = 9$
3. $2 + 2 + 2 + 2 = 8$
4. $1 + 1 + 1 + 1 + 1 + 1 = 6$
5. $10 + 10 = 20$
6. $4 + 4 + 4 + 4 + 4 = 20$
7. $4 + 4 + 4 + 4 = 16$
8. $5 + 5 + 5 + 5 + 5 + 5 + 5 = 35$

9. $3 + 3 + 3 + 3 + 3 + 3 + 3$
   $+ 3 + 3 = 27$
10. $6 + 6 + 6 + 6 + 6 + 6$
    $+ 6 + 6 = 48$

PRACTICE EXERCISE 2.1

1. $1 \times 6 = 6$
2. $3 \times 2 = 6$
3. $2 \times 4 = 8$
4. $3 \times 5 = 15$
5. $6 \times 5 = 30$

PRACTICE EXERCISE 2.2

1. $5 \times 2 = 10$
2. $3 \times 6 = 18$
3. $4 \times 3 = 12$
4. $5 \times 6 = 30$
5. $7 \times 3 = 21$

PRACTICE EXERCISE 3.1

1. $5 \times 2 = 10$

2. $4 \times 3 = 12$
3. $2 \times 4 = 8$

4. $3 \times 5 = 15$
5. $9 \times 2 = 18$

PRACTICE EXERCISE 3.2

1. $6 \times 3 = 18$
2. $5 \times 3 = 15$
3. $3 \times 3 = 9$
4. $2 \times 7 = 14$
5. $8 \times 1 = 8$

DRILL 1: MULTIPLY BY 1, 2, AND 3

1. 1	16. 15
2. 2	17. 18
3. 3	18. 8
4. 4	19. 12
5. 6	20. 15
6. 3	21. 1
7. 6	22. 8
8. 4	23. 12
9. 6	24. 14
10. 7	25. 21
11. 8	26. 16
12. 12	27. 9
13. 9	28. 24
14. 4	29. 30
15. 10	30. 20

FUN WITH MATH 1: SPINNING EQUAL GROUPS

Answers will vary.

PRACTICE EXERCISE 4.1

1. $4 \times 4 = 16$
2. $3 \times 5 = 15$
3. $3 \times 3 = 9$
4. $3 \times 4 = 12$
5. $2 \times 6 = 12$

PRACTICE EXERCISE 4.2

1. $4 \times 5 = 20$
2. $7 \times 3 = 21$
3. $6 \times 4 = 24$
4. $4 \times 2 = 8$
5. $8 \times 3 = 24$

PRACTICE EXERCISE 5.1

1. 1 row of 5 = 5, $1 \times 5 = 5$
2. 2 rows of 8 = 16, $2 \times 8 = 16$
3. 1 row of 6 = 6, $1 \times 6 = 6$
4. 2 rows of 5 = 10, $2 \times 5 = 10$
5. 4 rows of 6 = 24, $4 \times 6 = 24$

PRACTICE EXERCISE 5.2

1. 16
2. 25
3. 32
4. 27
5. 5
6. 20

PRACTICE EXERCISE 6.1

1. 0
2. 0
3. 0
4. 0
5. 0
6. 0
7. $3 \times 0 = 0$ items
8. $7 \times 0 = 0$ cookies

PRACTICE EXERCISE 6.2

1. 4
2. 2
3. 9
4. 7
5. 0
6. 4
7. $1 \times 10 = 10$ pencils
8. $1 \times 6 = 6$ cookies

DRILL 2: MULTIPLY BY 0, 1, 2, 3, 4, AND 5

1. 3	16. 9
2. 0	17. 15
3. 3	18. 7
4. 8	19. 0
5. 25	20. 10
6. 10	21. 7
7. 0	22. 4
8. 40	23. 14
9. 30	24. 40
10. 6	25. 0
11. 2	26. 8
12. 4	27. 18
13. 9	28. 8
14. 8	29. 0
15. 5	30. 12

FUN WITH MATH 2: MULTIPLICATION WHEELS

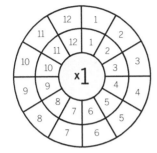

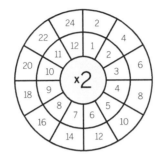

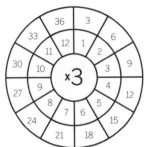

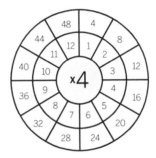

PRACTICE EXERCISE 7.1
1. 6
2. 4
3. 10
4. 12
5. 14
6. 18
7. 2 × 8 = 16 cups
8. 4 × 2 = 8 pounds

PRACTICE EXERCISE 7.2
1. 8
2. 24
3. 12
4. 32
5. 12
6. 28
7. 4 × 3 = $12
8. 8 × 4 = 32 candies

PRACTICE EXERCISE 8.1
1. 10
2. 30
3. 60
4. 20
5. 70
6. 80
7. 5 × 10 = 50 trees
8. 10 × 7 = 70 flowers

PRACTICE EXERCISE 8.2
1. 15
2. 5
3. 30
4. 25
5. 20
6. 45
7. 8 × 5 = 40 minutes
8. 3 × 5 = $15

PRACTICE EXERCISE 9.1
1. 6
2. 9
3. 15
4. 30
5. 21
6. 27
7. 3 × 5 = 15 pencils
8. 3 × 9 = 27 cupcakes

PRACTICE EXERCISE 9.2
1. 6
2. 12
3. 24
4. 36
5. 48
6. 60
7. 5 × 6 = 30 people
8. 6 × 8 = 48 cookies

DRILL 3: MULTIPLY BY 0, 1, 2, 3, 4, 5, 6, AND 10
1. 0
2. 30
3. 12
4. 16
5. 35
6. 18
7. 18
8. 60
9. 20
10. 18
11. 14
12. 24
13. 24
14. 16
15. 15
16. 30
17. 18
18. 70
19. 24
20. 30
21. 36
22. 8
23. 42
24. 20
25. 32
26. 16
27. 14
28. 24
29. 0
30. 32

FUN WITH MATH 3: MULTIPLICATION TABLE PUZZLE

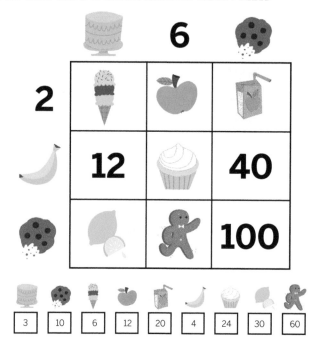

PRACTICE EXERCISE 12.1

1. 1
2. 3
3. 2
4. 4
5. 7
6. 9
7. 50 ÷ 5 = 10 boxes
8. 25 ÷ 5 = 5 containers

PRACTICE EXERCISE 12.2

1. 10
2. 1
3. 3
4. 5
5. 7
6. 10
7. 80 ÷ 10 = 8 players
8. 60 ÷ 10 = 6 hours

DRILL 4: DIVIDE BY 1, 2, 4, 5, AND 10

1. 1		16. 9
2. 3		17. 4
3. 5		18. 5
4. 6		19. 6
5. 4		20. 5
6. 5		21. 15
7. 2		22. 10
8. 3		23. 7
9. 1		24. 5
10. 6		25. 9
11. 2		26. 8
12. 5		27. 10
13. 8		28. 4
14. 4		29. 6
15. 3		30. 10

PRACTICE EXERCISE 10.1

1. 21
2. 24
3. 42
4. 32
5. 48
6. 63
7. 8 × 5 = 40 pencils
8. 4 × 9 = 36 students

PRACTICE EXERCISE 11.1

1. 3
2. 4
3. 1
4. 5
5. 3
6. 4
7. 12 ÷ 2 = 6 bicycles
8. 16 ÷ 4 = 4 days

PRACTICE EXERCISE 10.2

1. 28
2. 56
3. 49
4. 36
5. 64
6. 81
7. 9 × 6 = 54 doughnuts
8. 8 × 6 = 48 fish

PRACTICE EXERCISE 11.2

1. 8
2. 8
3. 1
4. 9
5. 6
6. 9
7. 16 ÷ 4 = 4 cookies
8. 12 ÷ 4 = $3

FUN WITH MATH 4: ROLL AND COLOR

4 ÷ 2 2	6 ÷ 2 3	5 ÷ 1 5	24 ÷ 2 12	18 ÷ 2 9
14 ÷ 2 7	8 ÷ 4 2	10 ÷ 2 5	15 ÷ 5 3	24 ÷ 4 6
25 ÷ 5 5	20 ÷ 5 4	16 ÷ 4 4	40 ÷ 4 10	16 ÷ 4 4
90 ÷ 10 9	20 ÷ 5 4	20 ÷ 4 5	16 ÷ 2 8	30 ÷ 5 6
24 ÷ 4 6	20 ÷ 2 10	20 ÷ 10 2	50 ÷ 5 10	28 ÷ 4 7
12 ÷ 2 6	32 ÷ 4 8	30 ÷ 10 3	6 ÷ 1 6	10 ÷ 1 10

PRACTICE EXERCISE 13.1

1. 1
2. 3
3. 2
4. 5
5. 10
6. 3
7. 9 ÷ 3 = 3 cookies
8. 27 ÷ 3 = 9 cakes

PRACTICE EXERCISE 13.2

1. 2
2. 3
3. 6
4. 5
5. 4
6. 8
7. 42 ÷ 6 = 7 cars
8. 54 ÷ 6 = 9 teams

PRACTICE EXERCISE 14.1

1. 1
2. 3
3. 5
4. 2
5. 6
6. 8
7. 42 ÷ 7 = 6 piles
8. 56 ÷ 8 = 7 minutes

PRACTICE EXERCISE 14.2

1. 1
2. 2
3. 2
4. 3
5. 4
6. 9
7. 54 ÷ 9 = 6 carrots
8. 63 ÷ 9 = 7 boxes

PRACTICE EXERCISE 15.1

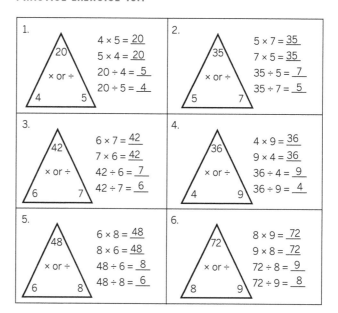

1.
20 / 4 / 5 / × or ÷
4 × 5 = 20
5 × 4 = 20
20 ÷ 4 = 5
20 ÷ 5 = 4

2.
35 / 5 / 7 / × or ÷
5 × 7 = 35
7 × 5 = 35
35 ÷ 5 = 7
35 ÷ 7 = 5

3.
42 / 6 / 7 / × or ÷
6 × 7 = 42
7 × 6 = 42
42 ÷ 6 = 7
42 ÷ 7 = 6

4.
36 / 4 / 9 / × or ÷
4 × 9 = 36
9 × 4 = 36
36 ÷ 4 = 9
36 ÷ 9 = 4

5.
48 / 6 / 8 / × or ÷
6 × 8 = 48
8 × 6 = 48
48 ÷ 6 = 8
48 ÷ 8 = 6

6.
72 / 8 / 9 / × or ÷
8 × 9 = 72
9 × 8 = 72
72 ÷ 8 = 9
72 ÷ 9 = 8

PRACTICE EXERCISE 15.2

1. 1
2. 4
3. 4
4. 5
5. 6
6. 6

DRILL 5: DIVIDE BY 1 THROUGH 10

1. 1
2. 2
3. 7
4. 6
5. 2
6. 2
7. 9
8. 9
9. 8
10. 6
11. 5
12. 9
13. 3
14. 2
15. 6
16. 1
17. 7
18. 4
19. 7
20. 2
21. 9
22. 10
23. 4
24. 6
25. 8
26. 4
27. 10
28. 9
29. 8
30. 9

FUN WITH MATH 5: MULTIPLICATION
AND DIVISION MAZE

Start →	4 x 1 =	5	12 ÷ 2 =	14	2 x 9 =	8	12 ÷ 4 =	6
	4		3		7		48	
3	10 ÷ 2 =	5	8 x 2 =	4	6 x 2 =	14	24 ÷ 4 =	9
	42		16		27		8	
9	64 ÷ 8 =	6	7 x 1 =	7	6 x 8 =	12	8 x 7 =	16
	7		8		48		45	
10	64 ÷ 8 =	5	9 x 3 =	17	7 x 7 =	49	9 x 2 =	4
	9		24		7		18	
14	24 ÷ 8 =	8	1 x 1 =	12	4 x 4 =	4	6 x 6 =	6
	9		6		3	36		
4	36 ÷ 6 =	8	7 x 4 =	21	9 x 3 =	12	81 ÷ 9 =	9

PART 2: GRADE 4

PRACTICE EXERCISE 1.1

1. 2,000 + 700 + 80 + 6
2. 7,000 + 800 + 30 + 4
3. 10,000 + 4,000 + 300 + 20 + 9
4. Three thousand and eight hundred and ninety-seven
5. Fifty thousand and eight hundred and ten

PRACTICE EXERCISE 1.2

1. 80
2. 400
3. 30
4. b
5. 14 tens

PRACTICE EXERCISE 2.1

1. c
2. b
3. a
4. b

PRACTICE EXERCISE 2.2

1. <
2. =
3. <
4. >

PRACTICE EXERCISE 3.1

1. b
2. d
3. d
4. $60 = 6 \times 10$

PRACTICE EXERCISE 3.2

1. 7
2. c
3. a

DRILL 1: MULTIPLICATION AND DIVISION FACTS

1. 16
2. 8
3. 56
4. 6
5. 0
6. 40
7. 0
8. 4
9. 40
10. 36
11. 12
12. 30
13. 18
14. 25
15. 54
16. 4
17. 3
18. 2
19. 4
20. 4
21. 5
22. 3
23. 8
24. 3
25. 6
26. 3
27. 6
28. 4
29. 2
30. 8

FUN WITH MATH 1: MATH SEARCH

6	1	2	7	8	0	3	5	5	1
4	9	3	7	1	5	8	2	6	5
3	8	0	8	4	6	4	7	7	0
2	0	6	1	2	6	9	3	2	8
7	1	2	2	3	8	0	1	4	0
1	3	4	0	4	7	1	4	6	9
3	5	6	9	7	5	0	1	2	1
5	7	5	6	4	1	2	3	8	3

red	$(4 \times 1{,}000) + (6 \times 100) + (7 \times 1)$	dark blue	$8{,}000 + 30 + 5$
orange	Thirty-two thousand and seven hundred and thirteen	tan	$70{,}000 + 5{,}000 + 10 + 2$
yellow	$100{,}000 + 50{,}000 + 800 + 9$	purple	$(5 \times 100{,}000) + (6 \times 10{,}000) + (4 \times 1{,}000) + (1 \times 100) + (2 \times 10) + (3 \times 1)$
green	$(1 \times 100) + (2 \times 10)$	pink	Nine thousand and eight hundred and one
light blue	Twenty-three thousand and sixty-two	brown	$(8 \times 100) + (1 \times 1)$

PRACTICE EXERCISE 4.1

1. 270
2. 3,400
3. 57,000
4. 2,540
5. 3,170
6. 2,900
7. 8,200
8. 93,000

PRACTICE EXERCISE 4.2

1. 10
2. 100
3. 1,000
4. 100
5. 10
6. 1,000
7. 100
8. 10

PRACTICE EXERCISE 5.1

1. 180
2. 192
3. 472
4. 4,125
5. 2,436
6. 4,248
7. 3,694
8. 11,700

PRACTICE EXERCISE 5.2

1. 288
2. 682
3. 1,462
4. 1,431
5. 2,470
6. 2,448
7. 3,456
8. 5,292

PRACTICE EXERCISE 6.1

1. 200
2. 180
3. 480
4. 4,000
5. 2,100
6. 4,000
7. 4,000
8. 12,000

PRACTICE EXERCISE 6.2

1. 200
2. 1,200
3. 800
4. 1,000
5. 2,800
6. 4,800
7. 5,600
8. 8,100

DRILL 2: MULTIPLICATION AND DIVISION FACTS

1. 54
2. 8
3. 25
4. 48
5. 18
6. 56
7. 64
8. 44
9. 40
10. 121
11. 24
12. 21
13. 40
14. 36
15. 64
16. 5
17. 6
18. 12
19. 4
20. 9
21. 7
22. 11
23. 7
24. 2
25. 4
26. 10
27. 6
28. 10
29. 6
30. 5

FUN WITH MATH 2: TILE TIME

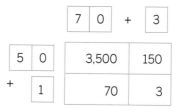

= 3,723

= 7,728

| 0 | 1 | 2 | 3 | 4 |
| 5 | 6 | 7 | 8 | 9 |

PRACTICE EXERCISE 7.1

1. 110
2. 105
3. 112
4. 848
5. 1,392
6. 4,984
7. 9,124
8. 26,565

PRACTICE EXERCISE 8.1

1. b) remainder
2. a) True
3. 4
4. 1
5. 2
6. 4
7. 3
8. 7

PRACTICE EXERCISE 9.1

1. 40
2. 30
3. 80
4. 40
5. 400
6. 500
7. 400
8. 300

PRACTICE EXERCISE 7.2

1. 414
2. 600
3. 968
4. 1,836
5. 2,562
6. 1,820
7. 3,552
8. 4,644

PRACTICE EXERCISE 8.2

1. 4 R. 2
2. 6 R. 3
3. 12 R. 2
4. 11 R. 2
5. 10 R. 2
6. 10 R. 3
7. 9 R. 8
8. 9 R. 7

PRACTICE EXERCISE 9.2

1. 4
2. 6
3. 30
4. 5
5. 20
6. 300
7. 30
8. 20

DRILL 3: MULTIPLICATION AND DIVISION FACTS

1. 9	7. 72	13. 48	19. 7	25. 4
2. 120	8. 64	14. 60	20. 5	26. 10
3. 20	9. 30	15. 63	21. 5	27. 5
4. 35	10. 121	16. 5	22. 11	28. 11
5. 30	11. 28	17. 12	23. 8	29. 4
6. 48	12. 63	18. 3	24. 3	30. 12

FUN WITH MATH 3: MYSTERY PICTURE

Yellow	Blue	Black
1,400 ÷ 7 = _____200_____	2,800 ÷ 40 = _____70_____	1,600 ÷ 10 = _____160_____
1,600 ÷ 80 = _____20_____	1,500 ÷ 5 = _____300_____	6,000 ÷ 600 = _____10_____
1,500 ÷ 30 = _____50_____	4,500 ÷ 50 = _____90_____	3,600 ÷ 90 = _____40_____
4,000 ÷ 40 = _____100_____		
2,100 ÷ 10 = _____210_____		
5,400 ÷ 90 = _____60_____		

70	300	90	70	90	300	90	70	300	90	70	70	300	90	70
300	90	70	90	300	200	20	50	100	210	300	90	70	300	90
70	300	90	60	200	20	50	100	210	60	50	20	90	70	300
90	300	200	20	50	100	210	60	200	20	50	100	210	90	70
70	90	60	210	100	50	20	200	60	210	100	50	20	300	90
300	200	20	50	100	160	210	60	210	10	200	20	50	100	70
90	210	60	200	20	40	50	100	60	160	210	200	20	50	300
70	200	20	50	100	210	60	200	50	50	20	100	210	60	70
300	60	210	100	160	50	20	200	60	210	10	60	200	20	90
90	200	20	50	100	40	210	60	200	160	200	20	50	100	300
90	70	200	20	50	100	160	10	40	200	20	50	100	70	300
70	300	20	50	100	210	60	200	20	50	100	210	60	90	70
90	300	70	200	20	50	100	210	60	200	20	50	70	300	90
70	300	90	70	300	200	20	50	100	210	70	300	90	70	300
90	70	300	90	70	70	300	90	70	300	300	70	90	90	70

PRACTICE EXERCISE 10.1
1. 426
2. 126
3. 123
4. 156

PRACTICE EXERCISE 10.2
1. 218 R.2
2. 190 R.1
3. 116 R.2
4. 215 R.2

PRACTICE EXERCISE 11.1
1. 16
2. 18
3. 45
4. 31
5. 21
6. 96

PRACTICE EXERCISE 11.2
1. 70 bags
2. 60 boxes
3. 65 pencils
4. 164 books

PRACTICE EXERCISE 12.1
1. 100
2. 30
3. 70
4. 100
5. 40
6. 500
7. 40
8. 100

PRACTICE EXERCISE 12.2
1. 400
2. 800
3. 700

4. 400
5. 500
6. 900
7. 900
8. 600

DRILL 4: MULTIPLICATION AND DIVISION
1. 30
2. 300
3. 200
4. 420
5. 500
6. 96
7. 720
8. 800
9. 110
10. 400
11. 4,000
12. 6,300
13. 2,000
14. 80
15. 4,800
16. 80
17. 11
18. 10
19. 2
20. 5
21. 5
22. 3
23. 80
24. 40
25. 40
26. 80
27. 70
28. 60
29. 44
30. 80

FUN WITH MATH 4: SPIN A QUOTIENT

$180 \div 3 = \underline{60}$ $190 \div 5 = \underline{38}$ $375 \div 5 = \underline{75}$ $240 \div 4 = \underline{60}$

$376 \div 8 = \underline{47}$ $152 \div 4 = \underline{38}$ $235 \div 5 = \underline{47}$ $318 \div 6 = \underline{53}$

$300 \div 5\ \underline{60}$ $150 \div 2 = \underline{75}$ $76 \div 2 = \underline{38}$ $450 \div 6 = \underline{75}$

$60 \div 1 = \underline{60}$ $424 \div 8 = \underline{53}$ $329 \div 7 = \underline{47}$ $360 \div 6 = \underline{60}$

$228 \div 6 = \underline{38}$ $525 \div 7 = \underline{75}$ $212 \div 4 = \underline{53}$ $188 \div 4 = \underline{47}$

$114 \div 3 = \underline{38}$ $282 \div 6 = \underline{47}$ $342 \div 9 = \underline{38}$ $420 \div 7 = \underline{60}$

$600 \div 8 = \underline{75}$

PRACTICE EXERCISE 13.1
1. 19
2. 32
3. 32
4. 35

PRACTICE EXERCISE 13.2
1. 20 R.20
2. 39 R.2
3. 93 R.30
4. 85 R. 50

PRACTICE EXERCISE 14.1
1. 288 seats
2. 336 hours
3. 375 pieces
4. c. Large, 30 slices
5. $4.50

PRACTICE EXERCISE 14.2
1. 39 cards
2. 22 packages
3. 21 tables
4. 15 days
5. 104 cakes

PRACTICE EXERCISE 15.1
1. 50 treats
2. 72 cookies
3. 60 fish
4. Lucy

PRACTICE EXERCISE 15.2
1. Stephanie
2. 624 supplies
3. $177
4. $125

DRILL 5: MULTIPLICATION AND DIVISION
1. 120
2. 270
3. 1,200
4. 2,100
5. 500
6. 1,200
7. 2,400
8. 2,200
9. 560
10. 270
11. 5,400
12. 6,400
13. 4,200
14. 800
15. 8,100
16. 300
17. 3,000
18. 300
19. 9
20. 30
21. 6
22. 600
23. 40
24. 300
25. 600
26. 700
27. 80
28. 70
29. 90
30. 90

FUN WITH MATH 5: ROLL AND ANSWER
2. 100
3. 933
4. 40
5. 804
6. 12
7. 45
8. 105
9. 32
10. 290
11. 122
12. 68

PART 3: GRADE 5

PRACTICE EXERCISE 1.1
1. 5,172
2. 19,560
3. 32,886
4. 38,425
5. 41,472
6. 59,592
7. 2,508 soda cans
8. $5,082

PRACTICE EXERCISE 1.2
1. 181,020
2. 68,475
3. 168,168
4. 159,771
5. 508,276
6. 481,023
7. 45,972 miles
8. $20,691

PRACTICE EXERCISE 2.1
1. 53,924
2. 69,012
3. 145,262
4. 71,622
5. 246,264
6. 221,562
7. 53,760 books
8. $165,585

PRACTICE EXERCISE 2.2
1. 677,322
2. 1,342,305
3. 868,350
4. 399,762
5. 3,125,172
6. 4,921,312
7. 91,250 pounds
8. $198,738

PRACTICE EXERCISE 3.1
1. Estimate: $600 \times 300 = 180,000$
   Actual: 190,440
2. Estimate: $700 \times 600 = 420,000$
   Actual: 402,408
3. Estimate: $800 \times 700 = 560,000$
   Actual: 534,486

PRACTICE EXERCISE 3.2
1. Estimate: $4,000 \times 100$
   $= 400,000$
   Actual: 507,790
2. Estimate: $4,000 \times 300$
   $= 1,200,000$
   Actual: 1,477,440
3. Estimate: $5,000 \times 500$
   $= 2,500,000$
   Actual: 2,257,675
4. Estimate: $5,000 \times 500$
   $= 2,500,000$
   Actual: 2,466,450

DRILL 1: MULTIPLICATION AND DIVISION FACTS
1. 20
2. 120
3. 1,200
4. 50
5. 350
6. 3,500
7. 70
8. 270
9. 2,700
10. 16
11. 160
12. 160
13. 32
14. 320
15. 66
16. 2
17. 22
18. 22
19. 24
20. 24
21. 24
22. 41
23. 41
24. 12
25. 12
26. 12
27. 12
28. 15
29. 15
30. 15

FUN WITH MATH 1: WEIRD AND RANDOM FACT

A $\begin{array}{r} 212 \\ \times 324 \\ \hline \end{array}$ 68,688	B $\begin{array}{r} 225 \\ \times 415 \\ \hline \end{array}$ 93,375	E $\begin{array}{r} 341 \\ \times 427 \\ \hline \end{array}$ 145,607	I $\begin{array}{r} 423 \\ \times 526 \\ \hline \end{array}$ 222,498
N $\begin{array}{r} 465 \\ \times 619 \\ \hline \end{array}$ 287,835	R $\begin{array}{r} 547 \\ \times 584 \\ \hline \end{array}$ 319,448	S $\begin{array}{r} 584 \\ \times 619 \\ \hline \end{array}$ 361,496	T $\begin{array}{r} 642 \\ \times 514 \\ \hline \end{array}$ 329,988
U $\begin{array}{r} 636 \\ \times 624 \\ \hline \end{array}$ 396,864	W $\begin{array}{r} 727 \\ \times 618 \\ \hline \end{array}$ 449,286	Y $\begin{array}{r} 827 \\ \times 299 \\ \hline \end{array}$ 247,273	

A
68,688

S   T   R   A   W   B   E   R   R   Y
361,496 329,988 319,446 68,688 449,286 93,375 145,607 319,448 319,448 247,273

I   S   N   '   T   A
222,498 361,496 287,835 329,988 68,688

B   E   R   R   Y   ,   B   U   T   A
93,375 145,607 319,448 319,448 247,273   93,375 396,864 329,988   68,688

B   A   N   A   N   A   I   S !
93,375 68,688 287,835 68,688 287,835 68,688   222,498 361,496

PRACTICE EXERCISE 4.1

1. 4,100
2. 41,000
3. 5,000,000
4. 2,070
5. 207,000
6. 9,900
7. 99,000
8. 990,000

PRACTICE EXERCISE 4.2

1. 400
2. 40
3. 4
4. 99
5. 9.9
6. 0.99
7. 5.75
8. 0.818

PRACTICE EXERCISE 5.1

1. 19 R. 32
2. 22 R. 4
3. 20 R. 3
4. 14 R. 20

PRACTICE EXERCISE 5.2

1. 32 R. 3
2. 12 R. 44
3. 32 R. 3
4. 41 R. 11

PRACTICE EXERCISE 6.1

1. 167 R. 18
2. 68
3. 57 R. 30
4. 301 R. 18
5. 54 R. 22
6. 186 R. 38
7. 251 prizes
8. 8 flowers

PRACTICE EXERCISE 6.2

1. 15 R. 14
2. 28 R. 112
3. 9 R. 390
4. 10 R. 339
5. 12 R. 291
6. 30 R. 7
7. 36 bicycles
8. 13 containers

DRILL 2: MULTIPLICATION AND DIVISION FACTS

1. 780
2. 7,800
3. 5,530
4. 6,000
5. 8,800
6. 5,100
7. 230
8. 2,300
9. 460
10. 46,000
11. 640
12. 7,800
13. 8,000
14. 640
15. 64,000
16. 27.10
17. 2.71
18. 89.9
19. 8.99
20. 270
21. 27
22. 2.7
23. 9.9
24. 26.2
25. 1.95
26. 36
27. 3.6
28. 39
29. 3.9
30. 3.9

FUN WITH MATH 2: MATH SEARCH

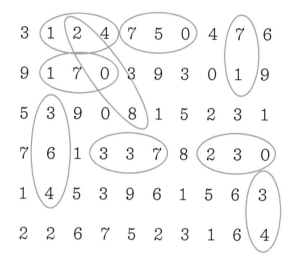

$355 \div 5 = 71$

$920 \div 4 = 230$

$2,184 \div 6 = 364$

$7,414 \div 22 = 337$

$5,616 \div 27 = 208$

$1,116 \div 9 = 124$

$1,700 \div 10 = 170$

$5,250 \div 7 = 750$

$1,156 \div 34 = 34$

PRACTICE EXERCISE 7.1

1. Estimate: $7,000 \div 7 = 1,000$
   Actual: 977
2. Estimate: $8,000 \div 8 = 1,000$
   Actual: 981
3. Estimate: $5,000 \div 5 = 1,000$
   Actual: 991
4. Estimate: $5,000 \div 2 = 2,500$
   Actual: 2,618

PRACTICE EXERCISE 7.2

1. Estimate: $4,500 \div 5 = 900$
   Actual: 908
2. Estimate: $6,400 \div 8 = 800$
   Actual: 818
3. Estimate: $3,500 \div 5 = 700$
   Actual: 699
4. Estimate: $3,500 \div 5 = 700$
   Actual: 723

PRACTICE EXERCISE 8.1

1. 0.4
2. 2
3. 2.1
4. 4.8
5. 6.4
6. 6.3
7. 1.5 pounds
8. $2.80

PRACTICE EXERCISE 8.2

1. 4.8
2. 27.5
3. 25.5
4. 9.6
5. 44.1
6. 36.81
7. 1.32 pounds
8. $19.76

PRACTICE EXERCISE 9.1

1. 6.6
2. 17.6
3. 42.6
4. 66.8
5. 162.8
6. 674.1
7. He is not correct. The
   correct answer is 8.4.
8. $18

PRACTICE EXERCISE 9.2

1. 121
2. 45
3. 62.51
4. 37.12
5. 375.96
6. 330
7. 441.6 inches
8. 134.4 square meters

DRILL 3: MULTIPLYING ONE-DIGIT WHOLE NUMBERS BY DECIMALS

1. 3.9
2. 45.9
3. 6.0
4. 16.8
5. 21.6
6. 48.6
7. 14.8
8. 20.0
9. 64.8
10. 30.5
11. 16.2
12. 6.2
13. 9.3
14. 12.6
15. 72.0
16. 12.6
17. 6.6
18. 63.7
19. 5.7
20. 47.0
21. 72.8
22. 15.6
23. 28.2
24. 21.7
25. 8.0
26. 18.2
27. 32.0
28. 25.5
29. 18.6
30. 15.6

FUN WITH MATH 3: TRUE OR FALSE CHALLENGE

True

$1.2 \times 1,000 = 1,200$

$5.6 \times 10 = 56$

$33 \times 0.3 = 9.9$

False

$6.5 \times 10 = 0.65$

$42 \times 0.5 = 2.1$

$48 \times 0.8 = 384$

PRACTICE EXERCISE 10.1

1. 0.08
2. 0.14
3. 0.36
4. 0.42
5. 0.18
6. 0.30
7. 3.5 miles
8. 11.56 in^2

PRACTICE EXERCISE 10.2

1. 2.64
2. 8.32
3. 8.775
4. 21.253
5. 20.835
6. 72.85
7. 1,239.04 yds^2
8. 3.25 yds^2

PRACTICE EXERCISE 11.1

1. 12.1
2. 0.24
3. 2.34
4. 7.8
5. 2.1
6. 32.2
7. $12.75
8. $12.50

PRACTICE EXERCISE 11.2

1. 2.9
2. 1.2
3. 4.1
4. 0.48
5. 1.45
6. 0.94
7. $0.92
8. 3.4 liters

PRACTICE EXERCISE 12.1

1. 2.45
2. 2.32
3. 0.715
4. 2.91
5. 14.72
6. 10.725
7. 141.74 grams
8. 0.9 ounces

PRACTICE EXERCISE 12.2

1. 1.98
2. 3.855
3. 1.34
4. 0.08
5. 0.14
6. 0.0075
7. 1.46 acres
8. 1.675 kilograms

DRILL 4: DIVIDING DECIMALS BY WHOLE NUMBERS

1. 1.2	11. 8.1	21. 0.4
2. 0.7	12. 0.5	22. 0.2
3. 4.1	13. 0.6	23. 0.04
4. 3.1	14. 0.3	24. 3.2
5. 0.6	15. 0.9	25. 0.03
6. 0.6	16. 0.6	26. 0.5
7. 0.9	17. 0.8	27. 3.2
8. 0.6	18. 0.03	28. 0.5
9. 0.4	19. 0.5	29. 0.7
10. 0.7	20. 0.7	30. 0.3

FUN WITH MATH 4: DECIMAL FUN

1. 0.84 ÷ 4 = 0.21 F	2. 0.24 ÷ 4 = 0.04 J	3. 47.7 ÷ 6 = 7.95 L
4. 4.7 ÷ 2 = 2.35 H	5. 0.50 ÷ 5 = 0.10 E	6. 0.68 ÷ 4 = 0.017 Y
7. 0.96 ÷ 4 = 0.24 I	8. 0.54 ÷ 6 = 0.09 S	

J	E	L	L	Y	F	I	S	H
0.04	0.10	7.95	7.95	0.017	0.21	0.24	0.09	2.35

PRACTICE EXERCISE 13.1
1. 100
2. 200
3. 300
4. 500
5. 700
6. 800

PRACTICE EXERCISE 14.1
1. 82.5
2. 194
3. 460
4. 13.75
5. 14,125
6. 1,440

PRACTICE EXERCISE 15.1
1. 10
2. 0.1
3. 0.1
4. b
5. d

PRACTICE EXERCISE 13.2
1. 20
2. 40
3. 60
4. 70
5. 10
6. 90

PRACTICE EXERCISE 14.2
1. 1,480
2. 7,550
3. 29,100
4. 9,500
5. 972.5
6. 333.33

PRACTICE EXERCISE 15.2
1. 10
2. 0.10
3. 0.10
4. c
5. b

DRILL 5: MULTIPLYING AND DIVIDING ONE-DIGIT WHOLE NUMBERS BY DECIMALS
1. 4.6
2. 2.4
3. 0.0016
4. 2.7
5. 0.0015
6. 3.6
7. 0.0008
8. 0.0063
9. 8.4
10. 5.4
11. 0.0049
12. 3.2
13. 0.0025
14. 0.025
15. 0.18
16. 0.8
17. 0.4
18. 0.08
19. 0.7
20. 0.6
21. 0.8
22. 0.4
23. 0.3
24. 0.5
25. 0.09
26. 0.07
27. 2.1
28. 0.9
29. 0.05
30. 1.8

FUN WITH MATH 5: SUDOKU

3.1 × 0.5 ___ 1_5.5	0.6 × 2 ___ 1._2_	2.2 × 2 ___ 4._4_	0.7 × 0.9 ___ 0.6_3_
$0.8\overline{)2.4}$ → 3	$0.8\overline{)3.2}$ → 4	$2.5\overline{)5}$ → 2	$6.3\overline{)6.3}$ → 1
0.7 × 0.6 ___ 0._4_2	3 × 0.5 ___ _1_.5	6 × 0.6 ___ _3_.6	0.4 × 0.6 ___ 0._2_4
$3.2\overline{)6.4}$ → 2	$1.3\overline{)3.9}$ → 3	$0.7\overline{)0.7}$ → 1	$0.9\overline{)0.36}$ → 4

TIMES TABLE

X	1	2	3	4	5	6	7	8	9	10	11	12
1	1	2	3	4	5	6	7	8	9	10	11	12
2	2	4	6	8	10	12	14	16	18	20	22	24
3	3	6	9	12	15	18	21	24	27	30	33	36
4	4	8	12	16	20	24	28	32	36	40	44	48
5	5	10	15	20	25	30	42	40	45	50	55	60
6	6	12	18	24	30	36	49	48	54	60	66	72
7	7	14	21	28	35	42	49	56	63	70	77	84
8	8	16	24	32	40	48	56	64	72	80	88	96
9	9	18	27	36	45	54	63	72	81	90	99	108
10	10	20	30	40	50	60	70	80	90	100	110	120
11	11	22	33	44	55	66	77	88	99	110	121	132
12	12	24	36	48	60	72	84	96	108	120	132	144

INDEX OF SKILL AREAS

- Base-10 numerals
- Commutative property
- Comparisons
- Composite
- Decimals
- Dividend
- Division
- Divisor
- Equations
- Factors
- Hundredths
- Long division
- Long multiplication
- Multiplication
- Multiplication by 0
- Number sense
- Patterns
- Place value
- Powers of 10
- Prime
- Product
- Quotient
- Remainders
- Repeated addition
- Times table

ABOUT THE AUTHOR

 **Kelly Malloy, MS,** is currently a fourth-grade elementary teacher in northern Nevada. She has been teaching for more than ten years and previously taught the third, fourth, and seventh grades. Kelly received her bachelor's degree in accounting and her master's in education from the University of Nevada, Reno. When she is not teaching, Kelly spends time helping other teachers through her blog, An Apple for the Teacher. She is also the mom of six boys ranging in ages from fifteen to twenty-eight.

CPSIA information can be obtained
at www.ICGtesting.com
Printed in the USA
JSHW012231151121
20501JS00006B/41